# Humeirah

**A Story of Existence, Beauty and Wisdom**

Sabah Carrim

ISBN: 9789671107409

Ripples Publishing, 2022

Originally published by Ripples Publishing, India, 2012
Ripples Publishing is the publishing wing of Ripples Learning Services, Bangalore
No. 12, 1st Main Road, K. R. Garden, Koramangala Industrial Extension, Bangalore
560095, India



Perpustakaan Negara Malaysia/Cataloguing-in-Publication Data
Humeirah/Sabah Carrim

To Humeirah:

My cosmos amid the chaos.

### The Vast Pit of Life

The vast pit of life stinks of misunderstandings
Deeper, the stench of superficiality increases
& when you think you've reached the bottom
torment & fear fill your bosom
for, lying there, is a soft pile of decayed gossip

Stepping on it plunges you further beneath
The vast pit of life is a sanctuary of oppressed heat
where white is black, & bad, good
where men & women prosper in falsehood

Suddenly the pit lights up & man is happy:
"God has finally heard me!"
But as he looks around & sees the filth
his joy is put to an end through his own guilt

In vain he looks for a support to cling to
Otherwise, into the gloom!
So, he sticks his palms into the sides of the pit
but recoils instinctively: his hands are musty;
he touched the slime of false dignity

In the pit, rain falls heavily
(Water can clean the dirt, finally)
But there is never an end to waste
& as the water carries the dirt
the man is drenched;
his clothes have aspirated the mud

Is there an end to this dreadful pit? he wonders
The skies bellow: Of course!
Do you want to be unfair and get there faster?
Yes! cries he, in despair
His descent accelerates
Life's given a different taste
Time flies, he gets there as promised
but warnings are never complete
& nobody's trustworthy
His final enemy awaits: Death

"Who, surprised and horrified by the fantastic tumult of her drives (for she was made to believe that a well-adjusted normal woman has a...divine composure), hasn't accused herself of being a monster? Who, feeling a funny desire stirring inside her (to sing, to write, to dare to speak, in short, to bring out something new), hasn't thought she was sick? Well, her shameful sickness is that she resists death, that she makes trouble." Hélène Cixous - *The Laugh of the Medusa*

"Admitting untruth as a condition of life: that means to resist familiar values in a dangerous way; and a philosophy that dares this has already placed itself beyond good and evil." Friedrich Nietzsche - *Beyond Good and Evil*

"Let us be on guard against the dangerous old conceptual fiction that posited a 'pure, will-less, painless, timeless knowing subject'; let us guard against the snares of such contradictory concepts as 'pure reason', 'absolute spirituality', 'knowledge in itself': these always demand that we should think of an eye that is completely unthinkable, an eye turned in no particular direction, in which the active and interpreting forces, through which alone seeing becomes seeing *something*, are supposed to be lacking; these always demand of the eye an absurdity and a nonsense. There is *only* a perspective seeing, *only* a perspective knowing; and the *more* affects we allow to speak about one thing, the *more* eyes, different eyes, we can use to observe one thing, the more complete will our 'concept' of this thing, our 'objectivity' be." Friedrich Nietzsche - *The Genealogy of Morals*

Praise for *Humeirah*:

*Humeirah* is a powerful philosophical novel, and a deep, eloquent feminist meditation on life itself, life as experienced in thought, and life lived in the quest for the meaning of one's existence. Those reading Carrim for the first time will be amazed not only by the sweet storytelling and the deft dramatic narrative style of *Humeirah* but even more so by the way she moulds thoughts into characters of their own: sometimes they figure as critics, disrupters, even villains.

**Chigbo Arthur Anyaduba (Author of *The Postcolonial African Genocide Novel: Quests for Meaningfulness*)**

This lyrically intimate portrait is equal parts wondrous and humbling. The reader will be drawn into Humeirah's narrative as she boldly shapes her journey in a closed and unforgiving culture. Married off early against her will, as her intelligence and potential are ignored, we come to bond with her amazing resolve. Never relenting, she continues to find herself through a most unique capacity to forge the most philosophical questions during her most trying times. This is wisdom forged not out of the confines of academic safe-havens but the mire of long struggle for authenticity against all odds. Readers are extremely lucky to have a new edition of this timeless classic.

**Ahmad Fuad Rahmat (Associate Professor in Media Studies, University of Nottingham Malaysia)**

# PART I

# The Search

# I

## -Freedom-

"To dilute pain, man seeks the company of those who share the same suffering." Humeirah

*Freedom.*

In the rear of her husband's new Mercedes, Humeirah was deep in thought as the car glided over a freshly asphalted road. Outside were signs and symbols of a Mauritian scenery: tanned and grassy mountain-hills that could be ascended in a few hours; wispy trees on the side lines separating tarred from untarred; shoots of sugarcane sprouting from fields of fertile-brown, and a sky, no matter where, a youthful blue or fiery orange with occasional dregs of cloudy abstractions that no film, no canvas could capture as aptly as the naked eye.

It never took much for the schooled and the unschooled to understand that lands were like people, displaying age through the subtlety of raw or mature vividness; and that this land was a mere cherub. It betrayed youth, freshness, unchecked ambition, and a certain naivete no matter the shabby, boisterous, and melancholy prevalence of jutting metal and concrete. It also didn't take long for travellers, if stifled by narrow roads and asymmetric planning to encounter the candid splendour of mountain-hills set in earthy amalgams of green, grey, and brown merging with flatter land—the chromic equivalent of sugarcane fields, road, fertile soil.

In motion, as Humeirah looked out, everything fused kaleidoscope-like and could put an aesthete in a state of trance, but somehow she felt nothing.

*Decades ago, women paraded the streets chanting "freedom" with fervour and passion. In the end they got what they wanted.*

*Was it because they were united?*

*Where can I find like-minded people?*

*But people who are united seek things in common. They seek to homogenise values and standardise conceptions of good and bad in order to apply the same formula to everything.*

*No. That's not what I want. What can I fight? Who can I fight?*

*My life, my existence and my mind are always dominated by scattered thoughts that have no direction, no meaning, no purpose. There's no one to share them with; nothing constructive to do with them.*

*Am I fighting to be a free woman, enjoy the same rights as men, have a say in everything?*

*No. I want something else.*

*Why do thoughts that bother me not bother others? Why am I not happy with things that make other women happy? Why can't I fit in?*

"The problem is with me," murmured Humeirah, conscious that the driver was within earshot. Her lips curled into a smile.

*How does it feel when a sharp knife penetrates soft flesh and vomits blood on contact?*
*What lies beyond this dark world? More darkness?*
*No. Everything will end when I die. My world won't exist.*

Humeirah's thoughts were interrupted by scenery that looked familiar. The car moved past Zeba's house, towards another equally ornate building but with fewer windows—one that had an air of abandon and disuse, apparent only to those who could see.

The driver swerved into the driveway and parked at the entrance. He was Vijay, a forty-two-year-old employed by the family for the last five years.

The sun was setting, the last beams casting strange shadows on the house. If one peered closely, one would discern desperate attempts to wipe off the dark coating of dust, inclement weather, and time. The dark coating was a sign of wisdom the bricks had earned; yet their owners had made them look like what they were not. "Maintenance" they called it; "disguise" it was, and a necessary means of consolation.

Humeirah reprimanded herself for being aloof and decided to be more aware of her surroundings till she reached her bedroom. So much was lost in being far away. She stepped out of the car and looked around.

*Five years have gone by so quickly and I still can't find answers. What is the purpose of my presence in this specific place and time? What is my function, if I have one that is, on Earth and for posterity?*

*I had hoped that every stage of my life would have something to offer, perhaps a new thought, a new insight. When I got married, I hoped my new life would give me a few answers to my many questions. But nothing's happened, nothing's changed.*

*What am I doing here, a being like any other, existing, breathing, living? Am I missing something important? Is there something in my environment that's important but that I can't make out? Why am I so restless and unhappy?*

Humeirah remembered that when she had given voice to these questions, *They* said it was the devil that had put her in the state and advised her father Gibran to have her exorcised.

Men in white kurtas and matching skull caps had come to her house to recite verses of the Quran, beseeching spirits, appealing to God, placing their right hand on her head, chanting more and more fervently, imploring then commanding the shaitan to leave her alone.

When it didn't work, *They* took turns hinting that it was time she found something more stable than thoughts that led nowhere.

Gibran understood what they meant. It was time for his daughter to get married.

Humeirah didn't put up much resistance at first, since young women of her age were also tying the knot. But getting married didn't make things better; it didn't keep her mind off the thoughts, and the restlessness remained.

*And yet,* They *seemed so certain and convinced that marriage was the solution to my problem.*

*Surely there must be some truth to it.*

*Maybe I'm the one who misinterpreted their message. Maybe I'm the one who has failed to understand what marriage is meant to teach me.*

(Numbers are known to have that effect.)

Vijay stepped out of the car, walked to the front door and pressed the bell. Nobody answered.

He tried again and again at intervals of ten seconds as if programmed to perform the function, while Humeirah stood behind him, aware, but not entirely.

*If life had to be described through music, it would sound exactly like this: sudden loud bangs of the same key, resonating with force and ardour, endlessly, deafeningly, forcing the listener to press her palms against her ears.*

*Or maybe it would be better not to play music. Maybe life should be represented with mere silence; dead, cold, harsh silence, because every time man ascribes meaning to something, he ends up butchering its essence.*

Shanthi, the maid, short, plump, and in her late fifties, opened the door. She wore a well-ironed dark blue cotton dress that was mostly concealed by a plain off-white apron. This was her uniform. Nobody had asked her to wear it, but these were the measures of discipline she had imposed on herself.

She stared at Humeirah while the small head of a four-year-old girl popped up.

Clad in a white T-shirt and red shorts, the girl held a dishevelled doll half her size against her chest. She was quiet as she peered at Humeirah.

The maid and the girl stood in the narrow doorway like two bold pillars, obstructing Humeirah's access into their world.

*Why do people stare at me? Why can't they soften their gaze on seeing me?*

Vijay returned to the car, relieved that Humeirah was now in safe hands. He had caught glimpses of her in the rear-view mirror, mumbling to herself. It was nothing new, but she seemed more contemplative and perturbed that day.

Over the years, he had grown protective of her—this woman who always seemed to be lost in thought. Secretly, he believed that she was suffering from depression, and that was what he could make of it, and since he thought he was the only one to see through it, he went out of his way to keep an eye on her; normally he would not have put in an effort.

Humeirah, Shanthi and the young girl turned to watch Vijay move away. Back in the car, he inserted the key into the ignition barrel and turned it clockwise—*the right way of doing it.* The engine let out a familiar roar and the car disappeared into the darkness of a weary day.

***

Humeirah continued to stand at the entrance of the house.

Although the maid's figure was imposing, the only space that existed was where her daughter stood.

"Warissah, come to me," she said, tenderly.

Warissah reached out and clutched at Shanthi's skirt. Hiding behind the bulky figure, she stared half apprehensively, half curiously at her.

Shanthi locked the door and turned to Warissah: "Mo gater, go and play with your doll."

Warissah scuttled into the small, carpeted room adjoining the kitchen, the doll letting out a repetitive sound by what was probably a metal bead inside, and of intrigue as she imagined it to be different things, often wondering whether she would get to see it.

Shanthi and Humeirah followed her movements to the playroom, the doll dangling with an ebullience that didn't suit the tense atmosphere.

The maid averted her eyes and fixed them on Humeirah: "You're late. I had planned to leave Warissah in your care and go to the supermarket. I must cook dinner, you know. You promised you'd be back on time and now my entire routine is disrupted."

Shanthi's cold welcome earlier now made sense.

"I'm sorry, Shanthi. Shaheen wasn't home. I was waiting for her, and it slipped my mind that I was meant to be back on time for Warissah. I'm sorry, it was—"

Shanthi sighed: "I will just have to do the shopping another day. In the meantime, I'll have to report the matter to Misyer Haider and tell him why there won't be dinner."

An awkward silence ensued. Humeirah knew that Shanthi never ran out of ideas and would come up with something for dinner. The wisest thing to do, she realised, was to walk away without compromising her self-respect.

A voice within her however pleaded: "Maybe Shanthi isn't so cruel after all. Who knows? People change."

Humeirah resisted, but the little voice kept begging: "Come on, Humeirah. Shanthi will give in, Shanthi will understand. People can't be that inconsiderate, that evil."

In her mind, Humeirah retorted: "But I've never known her to understand. She has always been cruel."

The voice chided: "Don't make generalisations. Maybe she will finally understand. Come on, Humeirah."

"Please, Shanthi. You know he won't be happy. You know how he is."

"Hmm. I'll have to find an explanation for the lack of food in the house. Sorry, I have no choice. I too could get into trouble. My grandchildren depend on me, and I need to make sure money comes in every month. If Misyer Haider's angry, I will lose my job and he will find someone young to replace me. Then who'll be there to look after them?"

Humeirah looked away. Once again, she realised she couldn't trust anyone, not even herself—nor the little voice in her head.

***

Shanthi reached out for the bolt on the front door to make sure it was fastened. Ignoring Humeirah, she disappeared into the kitchen to resume her work. Humeirah's meal had to be warmed up and dinner prepared for Warissah.

Noiselessly, Humeirah climbed the staircase of her house and walked towards the middle of the corridor, turned the knob to the room there, and nudged the door open.

Whiffs of a familiar flowery scent rushed past her—this was her scent, and it was warm and reassuring. But it was not always the same: sometimes her room smelled musty after being locked up for too long.

In this big house, this was the only room where she felt comfortable, so she spent most of her time here, thinking, reading, then destroying and reconstructing the ideas and beliefs she held. Occasionally she stayed for days within its walls, not wanting to speak to or see anyone, turning down Shanthi's requests to clean the room, and letting her in only to bring meals and remove empty plates.

After undoing the buttons of her shalwar khameez and putting it away, Humeirah slipped into a white negligee. She valued the smooth feeling of the cloth against her skin, its softness flirting with her body.

She climbed into the bed next to the only window in the room, stretched her arms and folded them beneath her head.

Shanthi walked in with a tray of food and saw Humeirah staring pensively at the plastered ceiling.

*This woman is good for nothing. Look at her lying there, doing nothing. It would be better to fling her in the streets where she belongs.*

In this world, only overt, perceptible actions such as cleaning, cooking, watching TV or playing sports made one look important and useful. A person who possessed a restless mind was still called idle, and idleness was nothing but a vice.

Humeirah's habit of isolating herself annoyed Shanthi, especially the unpredictability and lack of discipline in her ways. For her, everything had a predetermined purpose, and if not that, at least a fixed place that could not be interfered with.

When she cleaned and tidied up, there was neither a stain on the tiled floor, nor a spot of grease on the kitchen surface. Through her own initiative, she transformed a toilet paper tube into a vase for plastic flowers abandoned in a corner, organised toiletries of the bathrooms into plastic containers, and used leftover glue in the toolbox to fix a broken picture frame.

Shanthi didn't have to be told what to do and it was something she took pride in. Deep down, she knew that this was one of the qualities that had turned her into one of the most coveted maids in Haider's family.

Humeirah deemed such preoccupations to be mundane. If she had to do the cleaning—and only if she cared to pay attention—would she notice the dust. Even then, she would feel compelled to walk away.

What was the point of cleaning when the surface would eventually get dusty? There was something disturbing, she thought, almost cruel and violent about how dust kept returning despite attempts to reject and discard it, making a mockery of the person who fought it.

These differences in their personalities stirred a measure of unrest in the day-to-day management of the house, but there was nothing irregular or exceptional about it—it upheld the state of disequilibrium common to an existence, itself imperfect and imbalanced.

Shanthi placed the wooden tray on the bedside table.

Cold salad.

Chicken curry.

Two slices of brown bread.

Arranged in perfect order like in hospitals and prisons, the food barely looked appetising. Humeirah peered at it and felt too lethargic to go through the tedious process of biting, chewing, and swallowing.

Shanthi was about to leave the room.

"Quick!" said the little voice in Humeirah's head.

"Has Warissah eaten?" she asked, in a move to delay the retreat into her world.

"She will eat in a while. I am preparing macaroni and cheese for her."

"Her favourite, right?"

Shanthi was silent.

*This woman is wasting my time. She knows very well that that's the only thing her daughter likes. She is surely trying to change my mind about reporting the matter to Misyer Haider. Well, too bad.*

Shanthi walked towards the door and was about to close it behind her.

"Please don't bother to come back up," said Humeirah. "I'll do it."

Shanthi let out a loud sigh. Humeirah had told her how embarrassing it was whenever she removed her plate. It was the leftovers of meat and fish bones.

Other less unsightly leftovers, however negligible, were also a problem—a green chilli or pickled mango chewed and sucked off its juice, a cardamom or clove from a dish of biryani or pulao, or the skid marks of curry. Humeirah said she felt as if she was exposing an intimate, almost ugly, part of herself.

"As usual, everything is complicated with you!" Shanthi had replied. Humeirah refrained from explaining herself thereafter, and whenever possible, removed her own plate and made sure to rinse it before putting it in the sink.

Now, Shanthi marched down the staircase and slipped into the small adjoining room where Warissah was, and watched her play with Dolly.

Warissah feigned being Dolly's mother, feeding her, bathing her, and changing her clothes. A favourite role-playing game. Long ago, this area was a storeroom for empty boxes and old suitcases.

When Warissah was born, it was converted into a playroom so that Shanthi could keep an eye on her.

Shanthi wasn't pleased that in addition to existing chores, she had been assigned the duty of a nanny, meaning that she would spend less time with her grandchildren, two girls aged five and seven. Over the years however, she had grown attached to Warissah, and felt she was safer with her than her mother.

"No, Dolly, not *t'day*," said Warissah, shaking her forefinger in the manner of a school disciplinarian. "*Oni* when you're good," she continued. "You are a bad-bad girl, you hear me? You're a bad-bad girl."

Shanthi smiled and returned to the kitchen where she stood by the sink, grating a block of cheddar cheese.

*If Humeirah was level headed, she would stop her nonsense and start being useful. No wonder Misyer Haider can't stand her. Look at that poor child, neglected and left to herself. Who would ignore such an adorable little girl? God will never be pleased with Humeirah. She will suffer all her life.*

After Warissah turned one, Humeirah confided to Shanthi that she feared the power she could and would exert on her daughter.

"It's endearing to have a small, innocent, hapless child clinging to you with absolute trust, leaving her own precious existence at your feet," she had said. "It makes you feel like God. Any negligence on your part can put your daughter's life in danger as much as every act of tenderness, however minor, can put a smile on her face. How powerful a feeling. But what if I made the wrong decision and hurt her irreversibly? What if I jeopardised an important part of her development? No, Shanthi. I love Warissah too much. I need to stay away from her. I don't want to be selfish."

"Humeirah, you complicate everything," Shanthi had said. "She's your child and you are her mother. Your duty is simply to take care of her. Listen, you think too much. A mother is a mother, and cares very naturally for her daughter."

"No, it's not always natural. You don't understand. I can't help feeling this way."

Shanthi and Humeirah did not bring up the matter after that.

Now, as Shanthi watched the creamy yellow block of cheese grow smaller as it slowly disappeared, reappearing on the other side in a different state, angry and condemning thoughts of Humeirah distracted her.

Once the task was completed, Shanthi slid her fingers along the grater, removing the remaining half-melted cheese, and flung it into the kitchen sink.

A snap. The plastic casing of the grater had sustained a crack.

Shanthi regretted it, then remembered that it wasn't her fault.

*I have every reason to hate her. Misyer Haider could have chosen any beautiful woman to marry. He's so handsome, so rich, but he chose this woman.*

*Didn't they treat her like a queen when she first came here? What was the point?*

*This woman couldn't get the respect of the mistress of a household. Even Misyer Haider hardly pays attention to her.*

*If there's anyone who truly exists and matters in this house, it's me, not her, and everyone knows that.*

Then, Shanthi remembered that despite the undeniable truth of her belief, Vijay was the only one who didn't agree with her. He still went on to say that she was cruel and inhumane.

Was she?

No, she couldn't be. She reminded herself that she had the softest of hearts and couldn't stand the sight of a stray animal lingering in the streets, thin and emaciated from hunger and disease, and yet, she had overheard Vijay tell his wife Anjili: "What a hypocrite, she can't bear the sight of a sick animal but is so cruel towards Humeirah."

Was she?

*Doesn't Vijay realise how highly people think of me? Doesn't he know that my husband spoke the kindest words to me on his deathbed? Doesn't he know that I never fail to say my prayers before going to bed?*

Shanthi dismissed the thought each time, hating Vijay even more.

It was true that Vijay did not like her, and since he had to find a reason to justify his disapproval, he managed to single out an incident or two that negated her qualities. That's why the sacred love she had for animals was turned into a sacrilege and everything good in her was vilified.

But were those two situations comparable? Were they even connected?

What Vijay didn't understand was that red and blue had nothing in common; they were different spaces. It was man who had chosen to place them in the same category and single out their differences.

Similarly, the two situations were in deep contrast: Shanthi's kindness towards animals did not impose an obligation on her to show compassion for a human being.

No, Shanthi had not contradicted herself; she was not a hypocrite.

Yet none of this could have been explained to either.

II

# -Warissah-

"Our obsession with symmetry..." Humeirah

Warissah was quiet and well mannered, hardly cried or threw tantrums, and like many children who had not known more of everything, and were therefore unfamiliar with notions of adequacy or insufficiency, she was content with the little she was given. Under the circumspect eye of Shanthi and at times Vijay, both acknowledged by the family for her upbringing, she played in a corner with her toys, and as much as no one disturbed her, she did not disturb anyone.

She shared the same sharp nose and fiery eyes as Humeirah; otherwise, she was the exact replica of her father Haider. Wavy mounds of shoulder-length black hair framed jet-black eyes that, like a pair of overripe fruits, seemed on the verge of popping out of their skins.

Her intense gaze projected a mixture of sadness and innocence. She was the quiet and docile child you wanted to pick up and cuddle, so that you could imagine her clinging to you, digging her little fingers and nails into your chest and shoulders.

It was widely known that Warissah was precocious, and there were whispers that it was because of neglect; or what she had witnessed of her parents.

Warissah did not warm up to just anyone. She was attached to Shanthi and Vijay, the constants in her life, and on rare occasions when the former would leave her in Humeirah's care, she would play with her toys and eat what was cooked, turning a deaf ear to her mother's requests. That was why Warissah's reserve towards her that evening had not surprised Shanthi.

There was a kindergarten not far from the house. On weekdays, the teachers, Miss Monique and Miss Rose, took turns to hold art lessons and teach the alphabet. The morning ritual was the same: one of them would scribble the letters on a clean blackboard, and students would recite and then write them down on loose sheets of paper.

At ten, a lorry would stop at the entrance of the kindergarten, and a man would walk in with a crate containing pots of sweetened yoghurt for everyone. At midday, everyone would line up in the corridor leading to the bathroom, and pee in pairs, one in the urinal, the other in the toilet bowl.

When Warissah had to use the facilities, she would wait for the opportunity to slip in before or after the allotted time, so that she could be there on her own, convinced that the urinal was used to throw up in, and not wanting, of all things, to be in the vicinity when someone did that.

The sheer thought of a person peeing while another was throwing up, tormented her. It also made her wonder why so many children were sick daily; a thought which remained a puzzle. She couldn't remember the last time she had thrown up.

In the afternoon, the children would gather in an adjoining room, dimmer than the rest, and sit on the carpet to listen to a story read out by the teacher, and nap, only to return to the main room in the aftermath to draw or paint till it was time to go home.

Sometimes a helicopter's distant whir would compel the children to ignore lessons as they would rush to the window to watch it hover right above, crying out what Warissah mistakenly repeated as: "Alicopter! Alicopter!"

Miss Monique was a favourite. Warissah told Shanthi and Vijay that she was kind, gentle, and had a beautiful smile. Sometimes Warissah went on to describe Miss Monique's long flowy black hair, and how it fell in waves and bounced on her shoulders every time she moved.

Miss Rose, on the other hand, shouted at everyone, was strict, had blonde hair, green eyes and big cheeks that were always rosy. Warissah had never come across anyone like that and drew a connection between her teacher's name and the colour of her cheeks—*it made sense.*

A particular incident marked her. After lunch break one day, Miss Rose complained of a migraine attack, and waving a plastic container, said that she would distribute sweets to the quietest.

Everyone placed a finger on their lips and stayed still.

Later, Miss Rose announced the winners—the students sitting at *her* table, she said, not Miss Monique's.

Warissah didn't understand why no one put up a protest. Many a time she wondered whether Miss Rose had had it all planned because there were only so many sweets.

Warissah also believed that Miss Rose favoured Sandrine, a tiny girl who looked like a doll and had blonde hair and blue eyes. Sandrine had never spoken to or played with Warissah, but her mother phoned Vijay one day to say that she had an emergency and asked whether he could drop her daughter off at home after kindergarten.

On the day, Sandrine hopped into the car and didn't utter a word to Vijay or Warissah throughout the hour-long journey till she reached her house—a big white wooden building next to Balfour Garden, with a yard at least four times its size, dotted with tall trees with thick trunks. The mystery and dreaminess of its appearance had made an impression on Warissah, and she couldn't stop thinking about how similar it looked to a house in one of the stories Miss Monique had read out, so that whenever she played with Dolly, she promised to take her there.

But it was Suhaib, her friendship with him, and what happened thereafter that Warissah deemed the biggest puzzle in kindergarten.

Suhaib, one of the students, was perpetually punished and disciplined, Warissah recounted to Vijay, and on dropping him off in the morning, his parents would relate lengthy accounts to the teachers, of how he would act unruly in the house, toppling over or breaking this or that, giving them permission to do what they wished to him.

After they would leave, Suhaib would be made to stand in a corner of the class, facing an empty bookshelf and a bare wall, arms crossed behind his back, and Warissah would tell Vijay that his nose would be smeared or clotted with blood.

But what Warissah related did not make much sense to Vijay because she was not yet schooled in the rules of relating stories, so that what she said lacked a beginning, middle and end. In any case, what could he do? It was not his business.

Suhaib had big eyes, dull and phlegmatic, and was often absent from class. After his parents dropped him off at the entrance of the classroom and spoke to the teachers, they would whisper things to the children that would elicit laughter. Did the latter understand what was said, or were they already familiar with the rhythm of conversations and what was expected of them after a comment had reached a certain crescendo?

Warissah tried to figure out what they had said, to no avail. Sometimes, to not look odd, and when Suhaib couldn't see her, she would join the laughing crowd.

At half past three every afternoon, after Vijay would drop her off, Ustaad Ashraf would come home to give Warissah lessons.

Ustaad Ashraf was from Bihar and recruited to work in Mauritius by the Sunni Muslim Association to be the imam of a mosque, having the duty of leading the prayer five times a day, including Sundays. In between the rigid schedule, he was given permission to go to the houses of young boys and girls to teach them how to recite the Quran.

Warissah was always excited to see him. He was fifty and looked like the Incredible Hulk. She would watch him cycle up the driveway to her house, huffing and puffing, then get off it painstakingly, and with his foot, push the metal stand for the bicycle to stay upright, making sure not to let his baggy kurta trousers get in the way.

Ustaad Ashraf had a fascinating beard that was as long as the longest ruler Waissah had ever used. Whenever he spoke, her eyes darted to his lips, watching them move in all directions amid the morass of overgrown, tangled facial hair. The beard was unevenly dyed with mehendi so that it was quadri-coloured—a medley of orange, grey, black and white strands. Warissah wondered whether Ustaad Ashraf washed it with soap or shampoo and imagined him using a hairdryer to make it fluffy.

During lessons, Ustaad Ashraf would tell her stories about Prophet Muhammad and then move on to make her recite the Arabic alphabet—the segment she didn't enjoy because when she would make a mistake, he would tell her off. She just didn't like him—or anyone—being angry with her.

Before the end of the session, Ustaad Ashraf would place his hand on her small head, clasp it, close his eyes, sit up as straight as he could despite his permanent hunch, and mumble something incoherent which she recognised as Arabic verses.

"Shhwww...Wisss...Wiss...Shwww....Wiss....Wiss.....Shhwww," was all she could discern most of the time. Then he would blow on her three times while she would close her eyes as tight as possible.

Sometimes his breath smelled of masala, sometimes of stale milk, but usually the attar he wore disguised most of it. Every time Warissah would get whiffs of its rosy fragrance, it would remind her of fire. She was convinced that fire smelled exactly like that.

Whenever Ustaad Ashraf would appear before the front door, Warissah would run into the kitchen and hide Dolly behind the fridge. Ustaad Ashraf had said that dolls were "haram", a term she understood to mean that something bad would happen. "On the Day of Judgment," he once said, "they will become alive." Warissah had wondered what was wrong with that; surely it would be more fun to play with Dolly if she was alive.

But it never crossed her mind to bring it up because she didn't have the words to convey the thought. Moreover the way he had admonished her had made her feel that it was a serious matter—after all he had used the word "haram".

"Nonsense!" Shanthi had told Warissah after hearing that. "That ustaad is teaching you all the wrong things. I don't know about your mother, but I'm sure your father and your Nana will agree with me."

In this matter, Shanthi's opinion counted for nothing, and somehow, Warissah knew that. In the end, no one was consulted, so she continued hiding her doll, fearing the worst.

Shanthi spent the weekend at her son's house in Eau Coulée, so that Warissah either stayed with her Nana, Humeirah's father, or Aunty Ambareen, Haider's sister who lived with her parents.

Once in a while, Shanthi's granddaughters, Anusha and Valesha would come over and spend the weekend with her.

Anusha and Valesha were both dark-skinned and looked like twins, although one was seven and the other five. They had a thick coat of powder on their faces and as the day would go by, it would wear off and their normal complexions would reappear, so that Shanthi would take them to a corner and patiently dab a fresh coat.

The girls had the biggest smiles Warissah had ever seen, so that every time she drew the mouths of people in her art class, she would think of them.

Once, she extended the smile of the girl she had drawn from cheek to cheek and Miss Rose who was walking by, pointed at it, picked up Warissah's sketchpad, raised it, and shouted something incoherent. The children roared with laughter.

Warissah didn't like Anusha because she had "broken" her doll. While playing with it, one day, Anusha had combed Dolly's auburn hair rather roughly, leaving a bald patch on one side. Shanthi had to change her hairstyle by pushing her mane to one side.

In any case, Anusha and Valesha didn't visit often because they were uncomfortable in the house. It was Warissah's mother. She moved like a ghost, they said, so that they hardly knew when she appeared and disappeared. She also never spoke to them. Once, when Humeirah had smiled at them, it had seemed so abrupt that both had burst into tears—Anusha first, then Valesha.

"My grandchildren," said Shanthi to Vijay later that day, "are very good at detecting who is good and who is bad. You know, they say that children are innocent and spontaneous and feel things we don't. Well, let me tell you that both Anusha and Valesha can't stand Humeirah. You know what happened today? They saw her and started crying. I tried so hard to console them, but it didn't help. I've *never* seen them cry like that. I told you the woman is evil. Just evil."

# III

## -Our Desperate Need to Understand-

"I fear feeling too deeply, because the day I do, I will also feel things I shouldn't—things that will hurt deeply. Things buried deeply." Humeirah


Humeirah sat up in bed, eating the meal Shanthi had brought. Languidly, she brought the morsels to her mouth. The salad was dry and flaky, the chicken curry—heated and reheated several times—bland and watered down. The bread was fresh, but only an accompaniment.

Shanthi, normally a good cook, slacked off because Haider ate in restaurants and at the houses of friends, and Humeirah's opinion did not matter. Not that Humeirah minded; insipid food was what she deserved, she thought. Eating had become a way to be tortured. Chewing on something plain and tasteless amid the inner restlessness felt right.

This justification had suited her for a long time.

As Humeirah finished the food on her plate, she realised that she didn't mind the blandness for a different reason now. She reasoned that it made it easier to focus on other things and mull over what preoccupied her. It was relaxing just exercising her jaw muscles, munching, swallowing, thinking about faraway matters. Tasty food would have distracted her.

The new justification had replaced an old one.

The truth had changed...The Truth. There was a new truth.

*At every stage of my life, I am dead sure what I believe in is right, and when I find a better justification, I switch over to it with ease. Maybe what I feel about life today is also wrong. Maybe it will change to something completely different. Does it mean that all this thinking is a waste of time?*

Humeirah's mind wandered to the books she had read and the so-called truths and facts she had drawn from them.

*Is it possible that the volumes of prose that philosophers slogged to write are just interpretations and justifications that suit them, and only them? If so, are all conclusions we reach about life wrong?*

*In truth, is everything whimsical and subjective?*

A dark thought clouded her mind.

*What is the truth then? Is the truth constructed merely according to what suits us and what we find convenient?*

*If so, what can we trust?*

"Nothing," said the little voice in Humeirah's head.

The empty tray of food lay beside her on the bedside table and breadcrumbs were scattered over the dishes. Humeirah looked out through the window of her bedroom. There was darkness, and here and there the outline of treetops stretched out infinitely; somehow, tonight, the sight perturbed her. How she wished it was otherwise. How she wished for something more finite.

An olive white-eye flew to the windowsill, stood still, flapped one of its wings, poked its beak into its feathers and preened itself; then it hopped and turned to the other side as if peering into Humeirah's bedroom. With its characteristic owlish stare, the black-and-white of its eyes seemed so perfect, so painted. Eventually, it turned around and flew away.

How strange at this time of the night, thought Humeirah. Fruit bats would not have been surprising, but olive white-eyes?

Humeirah discerned a few stars in the distance. When she was a teenager, one of her teachers explained that, long ago, people had wondered about the tiny bright spots in the night sky and came up with the explanation that the Earth was wrapped in a black cloak that contained holes, so that light from beyond seeped through them. Later, people made more discoveries and unravelled more clues about the secrets of the world. The bright spots in the night sky, they said, were physical bodies far out in space, emitting light of their own. They were the stars.

*The physical presence of those bright spots in the sky did not change—how we thought of them did.*

*We need reasons for everything. We can't stand not knowing, not understanding. When we don't have answers, we draw conclusions about everything despite the limited information we have. The same way I tried to justify why I liked tasteless food, the same way the theory about the black cloak was conjured up—and that's how we often go wrong. But when will this perpetual search end? When will we face absolute truth once and for all?*

The reasoning and questioning were tiring, but thoughts ran through Humeirah's mind before she could open her eyes in the morning, while she walked down the stairs of her house, or brushed her teeth before retiring to bed. The truth was that she didn't wish for them because most of the time, they perturbed her; but like all thoughts, she had no control over them—they came to her first.

"You overthink everything, Humeirah. You should stop thinking and relax." That's what *They* advised her to do, and this is what she would say in reply: "I wish there was a switch I could turn off to stop me from thinking, but there is none, so I can't."

"What's wrong with me?" said Humeirah to herself, as she moved towards the full-length mirror in her room and cast a glance at her reflection. "Who is this? Who are you? Why were you born different? Wouldn't it have been easier if you could have settled into a quiet, comfortable and secure life like other women? Why are you staring at me with your dark-rimmed eyes, your stark white cheeks and your distorted body?"

*What's the purpose of my thoughts, my beliefs, my convictions? They might just be misinterpretations—or strictly my own interpretations. They will come to nothing when I die.*

*What's the point of conclusions when time is their immortal enemy?*

"It keeps you going, it keeps life going," muttered the little voice in Humeirah's head—but she didn't hear it.

IV


## -On Selfishness-


"There aren't two kinds of people: good or bad.
There is just one kind: good *and* bad! And the tension doesn't have to be resolved." The loud voice in
Humeirah's head


On weekdays, Shanthi would rush to wake Warissah up, give her a bath, dress her, prepare breakfast, and pack her lunch.

At half past seven, the sound of the car horn would alert them that it was late, and Shanthi would panic and speed up her movements. Vijay would be in the driveway, leaning against the car, waiting for the front door to open. Shanthi would then hand him a red-and-white chequered lunch basket that he would carry for Warissah while walking her to the car— Warissah had asked Shanthi for it since everyone at school had a similar one. On seeing him, she, with a sleepy face, would utter an enthusiastic "Ee-jay!", place her hand in his, and turn and wave goodbye at Ti.

After dropping Warissah off at the kindergarten, Vijay would drive back to the house, walk into the kitchen, sit at the table to have breakfast and draw up a grocery list.

Shanthi could neither read nor write but had a sharp memory she flaunted. While washing the dishes or sweeping the floor, she would make an inventory of empty boxes, bottles, jars, and vials that needed to be filled, while Vijay would jot everything down.

Vijay would then head out to the market in Vacoas where he would spend an hour or two walking from stall to stall, chatting with the vegetable and fruit sellers. When he would get back to the house, tired and sweaty, he would help Shanthi unpack and store everything away, while she would be reprimanding him for squandering time. "The shopping should have taken half an hour," she would say. Vijay would ignore her. It was the only time he had to exchange friendly talk.

Sometimes Humeirah would ask him to drive her to places, and while he never turned her down, he made sure that he picked Warissah up from kindergarten at three and dropped her at home. His duties ended late in the afternoon, but on Haider's order, he stayed back till the evening in case something came up.

Vijay's presence in the house made it inevitable for him to interact with Shanthi, and both exchanged views about Humeirah. While Shanthi complained incessantly about her, he unceasingly took her side so that the bickering was always the same: "She shows no concern for Warissah, Vijay," Shanthi would say. "Look at her. What do you expect of a mother? To take care of her daughter, right? But no. Where is Humeirah? Humeirah is lying in bed, reading a book, sitting, and staring at the world with that stupid frown that gets on my nerves. God has created a woman to feel for her child but this one doesn't feel anything."

"Leave her alone, Shanthi. She has done you no wrong. Poor thing, she grew up without a mother. She had no sisters and brothers to play with. Don't you see all this? She even got married without a mother to bless the union, and had a child so quickly afterwards. What do you expect? Nobody is perfect. Not even you."

"I am not saying I am perfect. You don't understand. What I mean is that she must take care of her husband and her daughter. She's just selfish. Listen, when my husband was alive, I took good care of him and cooked all his meals. I remember how sick I was one day, and how my whole body hurt. Still, I forced myself to get up and cook. My husband used to come back late at night—poor thing—after working the whole day, driving people in his taxi. Sometimes I would lie in bed, forcing my eyes to stay open just to be there to open the door and warm up his dinner. My poor, poor husband. I know he must be in Heaven now, and one day God will reunite us. You know how many people came up to me when he died to say that I took good care of him and that I have a good soul? Why do you think I try so hard to be giving? Because I want to be with him after I die so that I can look after him. There is no other reason."

"I am not talking about you here."

"I know, I know. What I am saying is that Humeirah is a lazy woman and a bad mother. You don't believe me? Speak to Raj. Raj will tell you. He says I am the best mother in the world and wants to be like me and take care of Anusha and Valesha the same way."

"Again, we are not talking about you. You are not being fair to Humeirah. You don't try to understand her. She's not a bad woman. I feel sorry for her. There must be something we don't know that explains everything. I have seen them together. Haven't you noticed how she tries to get close to her daughter?"

"Of course, you're taking her side! I know why. You are both lazy. What were you doing at the market today? You went at nine and came back at noon. Where were you? I couldn't start cooking without the onions. You always delay my work. I will report it to Misyer Haider, you hear. I can't go on like this."

Vijay and Shanthi would argue until one of them would get fed up, change the subject, or walk away.

***

More than once, Humeirah had overheard Vijay and Shanthi argue over these differences, and it pained her to hear what they had to say about her neglect of Warissah. But she felt helpless. She knew how *she* felt, and it was different from how Shanthi and most people did.

Then, amid these voices and whispers across walls and spaces, she thought about how people so close to her and within her entourage discussed her, how powerless she felt in overhearing them utter misinterpretations and falsehoods she ached to correct, but in its place, was compelled to feign oblivion and remain quiet and subdued—all for the sake of decorum and propriety, for this was the rule she had learned; the convention that kept her mum and shackled.

While they continued to harbour those feelings, dismissing Humeirah as cruel and inhumane, she too began to give in and believe it. The schism between what people thought of her and how she felt about herself was a constant source of torture.

Strangely, because selfishness was frowned upon, Humeirah had decided to keep away from her daughter, only to be accused of it. She hadn't paused to realise that *all* acts were motivated by self-interests, just that some tended to benefit others.

Perhaps if she had, she wouldn't have neglected her daughter and incurred disdain and resentment.

# V

## -Introspection-

"Indeed, knowledge gives one power....but no, superficial knowledge does, and with it the warmth of security and confidence; deeper knowledge only turns one into a cold and lonely human being." The little voice in Humeirah's head

Humeirah: If I could, I would waste no time. But there are chains; chains everywhere.

The loud voice in Humeirah's head: *You* have created those chains. You let them pressure you into taking steps you know will lead to your misery. They—your so-called loved ones—shamelessly utter: Go on, go on.

You don't pause to think about who their encouragement is meant to benefit, you or them. You think they have your best interests in mind. The truth is that they only feel good telling you how to lead your life because it puts them in a position of power.

But even if you know this, you ignore it. You always do what they say only to get a sign of approval because you are dependent on their love and validation.

Humeirah: No, the chains. I didn't create them. They are everywhere.

The loud voice: No. You love the chains. You complain that they deprive you of freedom, but you are not doing anything to break away. Whenever you are faced with truth before your eyes, you look around and ignore it just because *They* are telling you to do it differently. Every time you need to decide, you are more concerned about what *They* think so that you end up giving in, fearing their disappointment.

Humeirah: No, I don't want the chains. How do I get rid of them?

The loud voice: After giving in to their wishes, bending your values and pleasing them, you expect them to be by your side, sharing your moments of joy and sadness, and perhaps advising you again when needed.

Yet, look around you, Humeirah. You are alone. *They* have deserted you, and now that you have fallen, you still believe that something is wrong with *you* and not them. Numbers impress you, that's why, and *They* are greater in number than the single you. The world that held your hand and guided you for its own sake doesn't seem to care anymore. Are you surprised? Don't you see it now? *They* never cared, only pretended; they were merely curious, not concerned.

Humeirah: Then how do I get out?

The loud voice: Humeirah, you sinned the day you thought there was deliverance in following the herd. You sinned the day you thought it would be better to get lost in the crowd and obliterate yourself. You would have been among the few who saw light after extricating themselves from Plato's cave. But you believed them when *They* said you were weird—*mad*. And yet you are wasted. The most gifted souls on this earth don't always do what they have the potential to do.

Now you fight, but you only wound yourself till there are tears in your eyes and blood in your mouth. How long will you tolerate it?

Humeirah: I'm Humeirah and I'm free.

The loud voice: You are not ready, Humeirah. Freedom needs more work. Climb to the summit. It will be tough—and lonely. Lonelier than you feel now, and so cold. The only living creatures there are Schopenhauer's porcupines, and they shiver all the time. Yet they are wise and keep a safe distance from one another, lest their quills get in the way. When you are there, Humeirah, everything will become clearer. Break them, Humeirah. Break those chains that you have created and shackled yourself with. It's not late. Get out of the cave, go upwards, towards the sun...towards light.

# PART II

# The Party

I

## -Monsters of Moderation-

"Melancholy is nothing but abated desire." The little voice in Humeirah's head

Warm water—slightly above the temperature most would tolerate—flowed out of the showerhead onto Humeirah's body, washing away all that clung to her skin, forming a shallow puddle that trickled through tiny holes in the plastic lid that covered the sump pit.

It was two in the afternoon and the mugginess of a Mauritian summer could make one feel that showers, baths and water were no more than God's beneficence to man.

In Floreal, where Humeirah lived, it had never crossed one's mind to head to the beach since everyone was confined to the comfort and security of an urban existence. For them, the sea, the beach and the rest were for Sundays and public holidays, and even then, accessed within the parameters of safety and quietude. After all, everything had to get back to normal the next day.

For these townsfolk, the sea, the beach, and the rest, were for the others—those who took it easy, those who lived for the day, those who did not care that their children would inevitably neglect their homework and run outside to play. In the end, those who lived in urban areas on the island did not give enough thought to the sand, the sea and its saltiness; or to the birds, the boat and its boatmen; or to the waves, the wind and its whispers.

Humeirah stepped out of the shower, contemplating what was in store. Her sister-in-law Shaheen was organising the birthday party of her daughter Hannah. The faces of those she would meet that afternoon flitted through her mind: her father, her husband, her sister-in-law.

She cringed.

As she was about to slip in her bath gown, she realised something was not right—she had forgotten to soap herself!

After rushing through a second shower, she entered the bedroom. In the reclining chair by the bed, she basked in the effect of the leftover drops absorbing her heat, transported away to be part of another cycle familiar to man.

Today, she was absorbed by the notion of cycles—she had raised it with Zeba and Shaheen, wondering if they too endured temporary obsessions with thoughts and ideas when encountering them in books. There was no reaction.

For a while, Humeirah had been fixated by Michel Foucault's take on the *panopticon*, discerning manifestations of it in the manner systems indoctrinated and aligned the minds of the people making them. Then it was Karl Popper's coining of the terms *piecemeal engineering* as against *utopian engineering* that explained why people were resistant to change. Another was Tennessee Williams' Blanche DuBois—how her delicate beauty contrasted her despair and fragility; how her brother-in-law took advantage of her reputation as a liar to rape her, knowing that no one would believe her if or when she denounced it.

Now, aware that she might end up delaying everyone if she took too long to get ready for the party, she decided to stir out of her reverie.

Everything about the speed at which she moved and talked, she knew, was slower than everyone in her surroundings who was driven by lists and schedules, and worked from day to night, efficiently, robotically. She had negotiated with the thought of changing her ways but realised that it would interfere with the manner she engaged with ideas, and hence, tamper with the life of her mind. Every thought or belief formed in a short span of time ended up being superficial. No, there was no other way but this, and it came with a cost.

She walked over to the wooden closet that stood in her room, opened it wide and surveyed the row of shalwar khameez that dangled from wooden hangers. The clothes were pressed against one another so that only bursts of colours here and there jutted out: a green sleeve, a black sash, a blue scarf, a white collar, a yellow frill. The effect of various tones and patterns was overwhelming. Humeirah couldn't remember wearing any of them.

*Should I move them one by one to the side to take a proper look, just to remember, or at least, try?*

*Never mind. The memories won't be pleasant.*

Finally, she reached out for a mud-red shalwar khameez she had never worn but owned for many years. Where did she get it from? Who had given it to her? So much about the past had started fading.

She looked at her reflection in the mirror. The colour didn't suit her complexion, but how would it matter?

Humeirah had a generous flow of soft black hair that rested solemnly on her shoulders. Of average height and slender-framed, her movements spelled grace, and while peace and composure defined the outside, turbulence stirred within. One of the most striking features of her physique were her eyes. Dark-brown and almond-shaped, they conveyed raw sincerity, admitting no wiles, no ploys, but often because of that, let out the impression of vulnerability that misled many into thinking that she hadn't made up her mind about most things, and deemed it a weakness. Indeed she hadn't, the state of her unformed opinions correlated to her limited experience of life. Better that, one would think, than the stubborn and hence obtuse and cloddish appearance of confidence that the inexperienced chose to wear.

Peering at her reflection in the mirror, Humeirah focused on the large designs of magnolias embroidered in black thread waist-down.

*What if I picked an unusually simple dress to wear for the occasion, and ended up being the odd one?*

*It never takes more than a single act or a few words to change everyone's opinion.*

*How would people react if I started picking my nose or began undressing at the dinner table?*

*She's mad, They would surely say.*

*What if I blurted out something incoherent among perfectly clean, tidy and well-mannered people gathered around their sumptuous meals?*

*She's definitely mad, They would say.*

*Yet if my husband said: We Memons are the most superior Indians in the world. We are the most refined, the most cultured, and the most evolved, many would nod in agreement. Those who wouldn't agree would just not voice it.*

While looking into the mirror, she observed the contours of her body.

"You are me."

She thought about how everyone said she was complicated; about the thoughts that kept haunting her.

"I am you."

It had a different meaning.

*Did other people feel this way when they looked in a mirror?*

While slipping into the shalwar khameez, her eyes fell on a slim leather briefcase in the room; one of those moments when the subconscious would have sent a signal to pay heed to something unusual. The briefcase was shabby and worn out. It couldn't be hers since hers stored the books she was reading as well as a diary in which she scribbled a few lines almost every day, and on and off, random thoughts. Whenever she visited her father, she took it with her—Gibran hardly spoke to her anyway.

Humeirah opened it and found loose sheets of paper with a spatter of yellow stains, as well as booklets and thick books that didn't seem important, their bindings still intact.

Humeirah shoved the bag away from her at the sight of movement. Then, on realising that it was a silverfish, regained her composure. She noticed that her father's name was typed on the front page of a few documents.

She must have taken the briefcase the last time she had paid him a visit. Should she call and inform him? Or wait until she met him at the party?

But curiosity got the better of her. She concocted an excuse to justify the next move.

*I must know if there is anything important inside. If so, I'll call Papa and let him know that the briefcase is with me.*

Humeirah rummaged through the contents.

Buried beneath them was a book with a burgundy cover and inscribed on it was *Tartuffe*. A favourite of his.

She couldn't help reacting to the smooth leathery feel of the book's cover. It smelled so much of him: warm, slightly sweaty, faintly musky, mixed with the scent of his aftershave. But he didn't smell like that anymore; he used to when she was a child.

In those days, whenever he returned from work, she would run to greet him, and Kulssum who was employed to take care of the house and babysit her, would forbid her from rushing out: "You'll slip and fall and get hurt, Humeirah," she would say, but Humeirah would ignore her.

Before dinner, he would take a seat at the dining table, call out for his Hum-my, then lean over to put her in his lap, squeeze her palms in his, and kiss her noisily on her forehead and cheeks. She would reciprocate the affection in whichever ways she knew, and yet, feel unsatisfied: her hugs were never intense enough.

Gibran would carry her on his shoulders and walk around the house, mindful of barriers in their way, making sure that her head didn't hit any; or while lying in bed, lift her up, place her on top of his feet and move her up and down as if he was her seesaw. She called the game *aiyo-plane*. He could trick her into doing anything, whether to finish a meal or go to bed early, warning that he would never play her favourite game if she disobeyed him.

Then, one day, she grew up. It was a particular day; she was not sure. At thirteen, when she was tall and lanky and wore orthodontic braces like many other adolescents, there came to be rules for everything. Rules for sitting, rules for standing, rules for eating, rules for behaving. Her father had become strict and withdrawn, and she was no longer his Hum-my. Overnight, she had to learn to respond to a different name, and it fell harshly on her ears.

She reasoned then that she wasn't doing enough to make him happy.

Now, leafing through *Tartuffe*, Humeirah recalled other moments, pivotal in her relationship with her father.

There was the day she received her O-level results and rushed into the house waving her result slip, anticipating a change after he saw the As, convinced that he would spring from his chair and embrace her. But her father continued to sit in front of the TV, irritated by his daughter's loud and abrupt intrusion. "What's this? Humeirah, you must learn to be calm and express yourself moderately, this is so unbecoming of a young lady."

"But Papa...." she had said, too shocked to articulate her thoughts. With her head lowered, she walked out of the room.

It was easier to believe he was right and she, wrong, as he was schooled in the ways of the world longer than her.

But how accurate were these memories? How much was merely constructed and dramatised with the passage of time?

Humeirah had read that the memories we held onto were a medley of fact and fiction since we had added layers to them according to the vagaries of time, need and imagination.

Did she have better memories?

On her fifth birthday, her father had bought her a tricycle. Colourful plastic strips from the handlebars fluttered with the breeze when she cycled up and down the yard, which back then, had seemed wider and more spacious. The faster she pedalled, the more they fluttered.

She had cried out for him to watch her and put up a protest when he was not looking. He, more concerned that she would fall and hurt herself, barely managed to direct his attention on her, and cried out: "That's my girl. That's my Hum-my."

On Sunday afternoons they would go to the Botanical Gardens in Curepipe to fly a kite that would attract everyone's attention since it followed the order and colours of the Mauritian flag. Standing behind her, Gibran would hold her small hands in his, both watching the kite soar, and shower her with praise, telling her that she was "Papa's girl". Without a mother who could have further divided the attention, Humeirah had him to herself.

Nida, her mother, had died a few months after she was born, following an advanced stage of lung cancer that had spread to her lymph nodes. In agony, she had intimated how guilt-ridden she felt that she would not be there for her daughter, placing a burden on her husband's shoulders of having to raise her up alone. Gibran had reassured her of the saying that Allah never put a burden on someone that was too difficult to bear, vowing to look after their daughter.

When the promise was made, Nida had believed it. Little did she know that most promises were as misleading as words, since all umbras have penumbras—or shadows of doubt that accounted for perpetual misunderstandings. In other words, Gibran did not understand the nature and extent of responsibility expected of him, so that if anyone asked whether he had fulfilled his promise to his late wife, he would confidently say: "Yes." And supposing there was life after death, and someone asked Nida whether she believed her husband had kept his promise, she would unhesitatingly say: "No".

Now, many years later, in the bedroom of a large house, Humeirah reflected on the changes Gibran had undergone, and felt bitter. What could have caused them? Her father had shut the doors to the world of emotions and confined himself to one that had created distance between them.

"Fucking unnecessary rules!" she blurted out.

An image formed in her mind: that of a dignified lady seated amid a crowd of spectators, about to witness a musical performance on stage. Then, a violinist appeared on stage and began playing the most unexpected awe-inspiring tune. The lady wanted to get up and dance but remained still because it was not proper for her to do so. The music grew louder and more mesmerising, until the lady could not take it anymore. Finally, she left her seat, moving to the music and dancing her way through the rows of people; a desultory show she put on not for *their* sake, but for the sake of inspiration, for the sake of self-expression, for the sake of the beauty of life. She swirled to the music and moved her arms, legs, and hips to the rhythm of the violinist's tune. The world around her didn't exist.

Then several pairs of strong arms appeared out of nowhere, encircling her, stopping her in her movement, arresting that once-unstoppable dance.

They were Men of Order and Discipline: Monsters of Moderation. They were there because she had violated the rules. This was not a place for the effusion of feelings and emotions. This was a world where laws were dictated to organise, structure, discipline... and rule... overpower... and then subjugate... and standardise.

From that point onwards, Humeirah had to end her dance and leave the place in humiliation. This was not a place for her. *They* governed this world. This world was reserved for Monsters of Moderation.

Gibran was a Monster of Moderation.

II

# -The Impossibility of Change-

"What's unchanging about us is the absence of change." Humeirah

Humeirah continued to hold the book that belonged to her father. As far as she could remember, he had always spoken about two books: this, and *Far from the Madding Crowd*. When she was a child, they had seemed uninteresting since there were no pictures, the print was smaller than anything she had seen, and most of the words were undecipherable, but because her father guarded them in the drawer of his study where he stored everything of value, her curiosity had been piqued.

"Papa, I want to know what the book's about," said a six-year-old Humeirah one evening, as she walked into his bedroom and saw him in bed, reading.

"You must learn how to read, Hum-my," Gibran replied, motioning her to lie down beside him.

"Read to me, Papa," she said, climbing into bed.

"But you won't like it, Hum-my."

"No. Read to me, Papa. I'll understand. I promise."

Gibran smiled.

So, he did, but barely reached the end of the page when his daughter started yawning and rubbing her eyes. He pulled the comforter over her and kissed her goodnight.

Later as she began reading fluently, Gibran drove her to the British Council Library in Rose Hill and helped her sign up as a member. She kept her membership card in the drawer of her wardrobe, demarcating it as a space to store everything of value. Whenever she waved the card at the entrance of the library, the security guard let her in. Whenever she presented it at the counter, the librarian took a look at it, nodded, and let her borrow any book she liked. Little Humeirah was learning about the workings of the world, and many filled her with wonderment.

On completing a book, she would run up to her father, hand it over and tell him she was ready for the next read. "You're Papa's girl," he would say, caressing her hair or giving her a kiss.

Every fortnight she would remind him that it was time to exchange her books for new ones, and he would make time to take her to the library.

One day, while she was going through the bookshelves looking for the next read, he sat down in the waiting lounge and wrote a long letter to the Manager of the library, requesting an extension of their operating hours on Saturdays from 12 to 3 pm. Since it was closed on Sunday, he wrote, Saturday was the only day parents could bring their children to the library, but those who worked till noon, he added, couldn't get home in time to drive their children there. One month later, the library extended its operating hours on Saturdays. Humeirah was proud of her father, the influence that he could wield, and for a few weeks, didn't stop mentioning it to everyone she came across, including her school friends.

Libraries had always been a part of Gibran's life. He never failed to talk about a particular one that had marked his childhood—a library run by the Kutchi Memons at the junction of Louis Pasteur and Remy Ollier. He would describe the big table at the entrance where there would be monthly magazines from everywhere, including *The Muslim Digest* that recounted events in the Muslim world. On Friday evenings, he recalled, Bhai Yacoob, a stout man who donned a black fez hat, would sit at the table and deliver a sermon, recounting the story behind the ten days of Muharram, Eid-ul-Adha, and Yaum-un-Nabi, among others. People would gather inside and outside the library, and Gibran would describe how his voice would resonate through the loudspeaker all the way out along Louis Pasteur Street where people would pull out their chairs on their balconies to listen.

One rainy Friday, when everyone took longer to arrive, Gibran recounted how Bhai Yacoob had praised him for being on time, and that had spurred him on to read and learn more, and of course, attend many more sermons.

Now while Humeirah stood in her room with *Tartuffe* in her hands, its pages noticeably older, she recalled how her father's insistence on her being a member of the library had moulded who she was. It was strange, she thought, that they shared a passion, and yet, did not engage with each other about it.

Humeirah noticed a few underlined passages in the book and read one. Why had he underlined it? How had it resonated with him? Did it have the same meaning to him as it did her? She could not tell. Was there a depth in him that he was trying to conceal?

*But if he was really deep, he would have known better than to stifle those emotions.*

Humeirah read another underlined passage in the play, and turned a few more pages. She realised that it was getting late and she had extracted all the thoughts she possibly could from this encounter with the past, and as she closed the book, something slipped out.

Heavily creased, the rotund writing of the letter was barely comprehensible, but as she focused on the words, their significance dawned on her.

My dearest Gibran,

This is the last time I am writing to you. I can't take it anymore.

Yesterday your mother called. She told Daddy that she wants me to stay away from you. I thought Daddy would be angry, but he only looked at me and said: "You know what you have to do." He looked so sad, my jaan. It hurts to see him this way after the hardship that he has been through in his life. After he said that, I knew what I had to do. I know you won't be happy. I am also not happy. I never thought we would have to face this day.

We are in love. We are deeply in love.

I haven't slept a wink. I have been thinking of you and I will never stop thinking of you. I wish you knew how upset I am. I wish so badly that I could speak to you. But I won't. I won't call. I don't know who will end up answering the phone.

My jaan, they don't want this to happen, and we have talked about it before. Our parents must give their consent to our marriage, otherwise we will never be respected.

We have a whole life in front of us and we must make sure people wish us good if we want to live happily. I don't want to suffer because of their evil eye on us.

I know you will keep insisting that I am wrong, as you have done many times in the past. But please, just for once, think about it. This is a small place, my jaan. We can't just run away and get married like you've been suggesting. It will be a scandal. My father will be so ashamed of me. I can't do that. I just can't. I'm sorry.

Maybe they are right. Maybe you deserve someone better. After all, I am not a Memon. I am from a very simple and humble family. My father is just a schoolteacher. Your family owns property and big businesses. If I marry you, they will never respect and love me. Our children will be looked down upon and called "fifty cents" by people of your community. This is not going anywhere, Gibran. Please understand me. I have tried really hard to put up with this, but I just can't go on. You must know that I have always loved you and I will always think of you, no matter what happens. I wish you well, my jaan. I can only hope that you won't be angry with me… That you won't hate me…

My heart will always, always be with you.

Goodbye, Gibran… Goodbye, my jaan.

Soraya

The date was 25 June 1978. Gibran, her father, had married Nida in February 1979. The image of the reserved and contained father that he had turned into, came flooding back to her. What a contrast.

Humeirah tried to reconstruct what had happened. A few relatives had disapproved of Gibran and Soraya's union because of their difference, and that had forced them to go separate ways. Then her father had married her mother, a homely young lady who was his uncle's daughter. She was of course a Memon, and the union had been arranged by their fathers.

Yes, that made sense.

But their union was not harmonious. Humeirah had overheard one of her father's friends mention it, and that was all she knew. People didn't seem keen to talk about things that were remotely contentious, or made them uncomfortable. She read the letter again.

Who was Soraya? Was this really her Papa?

*My father was madly in love with someone but couldn't marry her because she wasn't a Memon. And what was it that he told me? That Haider was the perfect match because he was a Memon? But no… I am wrong. There is something else. Who is this man who seems full of passion? Who is this person who sounds so different from who he is now? My father? When did he put on the mask?*

She remembered how her father had reacted when she had shown some reticence in accepting Haider's marriage proposal: "Don't play with your future, Humeirah. The world you have seen is small. You are still young. You don't understand everything. I know what's good for you. Haider is the best you can ever find in your life. Look at those other men around you. They are barely able to fend for themselves, and they are not strong enough to face life's ups and downs. Look at Haider. He is a good Memon boy; he is well off and will be able to support you. I know Haider's father very well—we used to play football together in Champs de Mars when we were in school. Haider's *par, par* Dada and your Dada's Nana were brothers, so that Haider's Dada and your Dada were second cousins. When they came to Mauritius from Kutch in 1915, they boarded the same ship—*Canara*—and later, your Dada relied on Haider's Dada's trading licence to set up his first business in Port Louis in Queen Street in 1932. Your Dadi and Haider's Dadi were also best friends. They too arrived on a ship, but in 1933, and would tell us about the month-long voyage by rail and sea with stopovers in Mandvi, Bombay, Calcutta and Colombo."

Gibran paused, realising he had digressed.

"What face will I have to show them if I turn down the proposal?" he resumed. "Don't be ungrateful to Allah. If this man has lowered himself by coming to your door to ask for your hand, it is because he has found something special and unique in you. Be grateful and see how well you will be rewarded in life."

Humeirah placed the briefcase by the door to make sure that she would remember to take it. The new discovery about her father's past was exciting; as if she had gained a deeper insight into the workings of the world, and more importantly, into who she was; an insight into a time in history that would not have been recorded, and hence, missed out. With a renewed sense of determination, she took the wet towel from the bed and headed outside to hang it. In Floreal, that could only be done in summer, not winter. Then, her actions tempered, as she reflected on a thought.

There was a deep respect for norms that had withstood time: it was thought that they didn't merit reconsideration; it was thought that it was easier to follow them than go through the hassle of questioning old values, rebelling against conventions, and altering, or even reformulating them. It was thought that it was easier not to think.

*People, like my father, caught in that terrible mayhem, inevitably and understandably find it easier to give in, obey and follow rules, rather than defy them and create their own.*

*They are scared, because often, the price they have to pay is that they have to carry on alone, without the nodding and approving looks of the people surrounding them.*

Numbers.

Humeirah recalled the writings of authors she had read and loved, unanimous in claiming that a person's nature never changed. But Gibran had, she thought. He had put that wild, rapturous, and beautiful monster of emotions to sleep. A few people chose to call it "growing up", "attaining wisdom", or, "deciding to let go of their childish ways". For them, it was a mark of success.

Maybe her father believed that he too had succeeded in doing that the day he decided to put an end to the chapter of Soraya and start a new one by marrying Nida. Then, with her birth, he had probably let his defences down, but that had only been short-lived. Even Warissah, his only granddaughter, did not seem to stir anything up in him.

Or maybe Gibran had not changed at all.

Maybe he had just grown numb to everything after his separation from Soraya, and made a slow retreat into a perfunctory and robotic existence—because the truth was that people didn't really change.

In view of man's furtive battle to understand, to master life and its processes, and to do so, repeat the same mistakes, an average of seventy years of a lifetime was too short for something drastic and meaningful to happen.

Otherwise, why were the extensive commentaries by the pre-Socratics on human follies and foibles still relevant and relatable?

Without a doubt, Humeirah reasoned, books preached that to rid oneself of unhappiness, one had to identify the one factor or flaw perpetuating it. Then, they went on to suggest solutions and action plans, relating success stories of revolutionary transformations, thereby providing hope.

But most of the time, partaking of such reading only led one to single out problems—because all claims to solutions were farcical as well as falsely optimistic, so that one was stuck in liminal space, aware of problems, bereft of remedies.

Humeirah decided not to call her father. There was nothing important in the briefcase, save for fragments of memories that would have been of value only if they could have rekindled their relationship.

Here she was, with a brand-new image of her father, irreconcilable to what she had always known of him.

Humeirah looked at the clock, returned the book in the briefcase, and covered it with the stack of papers.

# III

## -Emotion and Reason-

"I have an innate desire to take my senses by surprise and expose them to the naked beauty of the world."
The little voice in Humeirah's head

Laboriously, the car moved uphill, and its passengers felt the engine's heaviness. In Floreal, close to the volcano, the roads were so steep that travel made stomachs churn. The driver was heading to Beau Bassin to drop the passengers off at Shaheen's place for the party.

Like many towns in Mauritius, Floreal was a maze of big houses as well as clusters of small and modest ones littered in their interstices, not uncommonly erected on slopes and subjected to the whims of weather. These humbler units were often bereft of gates or enclosures, barely managed to accommodate a small car on or by the premises, and were strewn along lanes that ended abruptly in narrow cul-de-sacs. While those who dwelled in these houses tended to be more aware of the presence of those with better fortunes amid their surroundings, the reverse was not necessarily true.

The more opulent houses of the town were surrounded by vast expanses of green land, but the view of every model, unique and intricate, was obstructed by high walls as well as neat and manicured bamboo that lined roads on either side.

Four people sat still in a moving car. In a surreal world that captured the extent of detachment among them, they would each be floating in a separate bubble, confined to that space, restricted to the thoughts on their minds, lost in a world of their making. There was violence in the distance.

The car snaked its way around the golf course of Gymkhana Club in Vacoas, passed Jumbo Phoenix and merged into the M1 towards Beau Bassin. From Belle Rose to Rose Hill, it weaved through a quaint cluster of single-storey shops that sold jewellery, kitchenware, clothes and toys from India, China and South Africa. Old-fashioned shutters of corrugated iron, painted in dark shades, covered the doors and windows of the shops. It was four on a Sunday afternoon and Rose Hill was deserted, making it easier to get around. The car took the roundabout near the market in Rose Hill and passed the British Council Library—a plain white building on top of Bata and HSBC where booklovers no longer went; the library had shut its doors to make way for modern means of reading.

The four individuals in the car barely exchanged a word during the journey. Haider was engrossed in a conversation on the phone, his tone conveying drunken happiness: Manchester United had beaten Chelsea. After hanging up, he scrolled through his contacts, searching names of friends he recalled being Chelsea fans. Finally, he found one.

"Michael, did you watch that match just now?"

Haider waited for a reply and then laughed mockingly: "You lost! Chicharito is such a champ. He kicked your ass! We will definitely win our nineteenth title. Wait and see. We will always be the best." Again, there was silence, as Michael probably challenged what Haider had said, to which the latter replied: "Oh yeah?", and with another guffaw, added: "We'll see. OK, Man, I must go now. Catch you later. Ciao."

In the rear seat beside Warissah, Humeirah smirked.

It was strange and uncommon for the three members who belonged to the same family to be together, heading to the same place. But they were attending Hannah's birthday and everyone in the family would be present, so that for the eyes of the people, it had to look like everything was at its best in the best of possible worlds.

Vijay was deeply engrossed with thoughts about his wife Anjili. He wanted to drop Haider, Humeirah and Warissah off quickly so that he could go home to see her. She was three months pregnant with their first child and had been throwing up so often that she had been admitted in hospital a few times where a serum was administered.

From the start, Vijay had shared an intimate and loving relationship with her and had the habit of filling her with the day's gossip about the family for whom he worked. The events and facts were not the same, but the conclusions were: Humeirah was sad and depressed, Haider was busy at work and out with friends, Warissah was a neglected child, and Shanthi was complaining about Humeirah and the load of work piled on her.

But life with Anjili was peaceful and effortless, and because of that, Vijay grew weary of the monotony and boredom of the consistent dose of happiness. He wished for something more; he ached to feel alive; he ached for chaos. Using the disorganisation as well as the silence and assumptions made within the family, including Humeirah's irregular requests to go out and Haider's to buy this or that, he would sneak out to visit Hanisha who worked as a maid for Zeba, the lady next door. Hanisha worked around his schedule as the two other maids on the premises were in cahoots with her—but as most cases, only in the beginning. Lately, they had turned against her, claiming that her immoral conduct could threaten their jobs and livelihood.

Because of these surreptitious but successful escapades, Vijay revelled in the thought of being smart, and very soon, exuded the air of a con artist who had mastered the tricks to beat the system. What he did not know was that everyone was already suspicious of his activities.

When he began to see Hanisha, he was sure that he would be able to conceal it, and if ever they learned about it, he told himself that he would disprove it by furnishing innocent explanations of his whereabouts, or even an alibi—Pravin, a vegetable seller in Vacoas and a friend, knew his secret. But no one mentioned it, since it would be embarrassing for him and for them, and even if they harboured the idea of doing so, they knew he would tell them a lie. Instead, they chose the easier route by talking and laughing about the affair behind his back, and that was the end of the matter.

It must be stressed that none of these people had hard evidence of his extramarital affair; they had merely *sensed* it and gone on to draw the appropriate conclusion. With little backing the conjecture, one could accuse them of being judgmental, but as in this case, the irony was that the accused, as well as their conjectures and judgments were often right.

Now, on the way to Beau Bassin, while calculating the time needed to rush home to make sure that Anjili was all right, Vijay was also figuring out how to sneak in a quick meeting with Hanisha. He could get home in twenty-five minutes, spend ten to fifteen with Anjili, and the remainder—another fifteen—no, he could do five with Anjili and have about twenty-five with Hanisha, and get back to Beau Bassin by half past five—just in time to pick Haider, Humeirah and Warissah up.

While Vijay was making plans, Warissah sat quietly next to Humeirah with Dolly in her lap and eyes glued to the outside. Humeirah took a side-glance at her daughter. What was going on in her mind? Were they the same questions that had haunted her when she was of her age? Suddenly, Humeirah felt deep regret for not knowing, and reached out to hold her daughter's hand, half the size of her own. But Warissah quickly withdrew it, as if her hands were musty; as if she had come in contact with something repugnant. Humeirah felt a pinch.

Her daughter's aloofness was normal because they weren't close to each other, she told herself, but soon enough, she found it hard to use reason to harness the guilt and rejection.

Her mind raced with new thoughts. She wanted to remember why she had decided to stay away from Warissah. When she was pregnant, she had hopes and dreams about how she wanted her daughter to be. For one, she wanted her to be different from the children she had come across, and more than anything, she wanted her to be curious rather than complacent towards everything. Only then, Humeirah had thought, would she be able to engage with her and show her the things she knew and had read about. Only then would she be able to bring her up the way she herself was never brought up. Only then being a parent would have had meaning.

Humeirah had often lain in bed, staring at the collection of books she owned, imagining reading them to her daughter when she would be older.

But she also realised one day that her daughter could end up not being all that.

What if her disappointment made her mistreat her child? More importantly, who was she to think that she had the right to teach her? Who was she to think that she had answers to everything and could guide her? Being a mother, Humeirah realised, gave her undue authority, and it felt wrong to abuse it.

In the car that day, she tried to remember the name of a writer, a thinker, or just anyone who would nod in approval and say, "Yes, Humeirah—you are right to think this way."

*Gulliver's Travels* came to mind. Jonathan Swift had once described a world where the state would take over caring for children from the time they were born. It seemed a better idea than leaving children brought up arbitrarily by irresponsible parents, certain of their formula for raising them, or who just didn't care to give it much thought. Swift just knew how much harm parents could do to their own children, thought Humeirah.

But that afternoon, no matter how hard she tried to console herself with these excuses, the restlessness and agitation remained.

Humeirah looked at her daughter again. As was her habit in the presence of both parents, Warissah had not uttered a word, and was still looking outside. From that angle, Humeirah realised that her daughter could barely see or be seen by pedestrians or drivers and passengers in other vehicles. What Warissah *could* see however, were probably treetops, upper storeys of buildings, buses, and roofs of other cars; maybe the sky. What else had caught her daughter's attention from that vantage point that she herself hadn't?

The car came to a stop. Vijay dropped Haider, Humeirah and Warissah in front of Shaheen's house and drove away.

Haider walked into the sitting room of the house with Humeirah and Warissah right behind. Hannah's mother Shaheen opened the door.

"Haider, Humeirah, come in, come in. Humeirah, I was told that you came home last Thursday. I'm sorry I wasn't in."

"It's OK. I thought you went shopping."

"Shopping? In this country? No way! You know I never shop here. Even if you pick the most exclusive shops, you'll always end up wearing something someone else is wearing. Actually, I stepped out to place an order for cakes. Fatima makes them. Did you know? I went over to her place to ask her to prepare something for today." She lowered her voice: "I wanted to speak to you about something. That's why I asked to see you that day. Listen, let's arrange to meet tomorrow, shall we? I'll give you a call."

"Sure," said Humeirah, wondering why, of all persons, she was being sought. Nobody sought her for anything.

There was a small gathering of about twenty people in Shaheen's house. The guests were elegantly dressed: husbands wore designer shirts that wives had purchased on their travels while the latter were dressed in shalwar khameez of varied patterns and colours imported from India, Pakistan, and Dubai. Humeirah looked around and became self-conscious, remembering the olive-green dress with colourful beads tucked in her closet. Maybe that would have been more appropriate.

Humeirah noticed her father and went up to him. He was by the dining table, engaged in a conversation with a man in his early thirties. Gibran turned around.

"Assalamualaikum, Humeirah."

"Walaikumsalam, Papa."

As was his habit, Gibran refrained from physical contact. It was an Islamic prescription, he said, that a father should only kiss his daughter on the forehead. This too, he only did rarely. On Eid and special occasions, in line with Memon custom, Humeirah placed the dorsal side of his right hand against her right eye, followed by her left eye, and kissed it.

"Humeirah, meet Saabir. He is the author of...of...how many was that again...three books." Turning to Saabir, he said: "Saabir this is Humeirah, my daughter. She is the wife of the gentleman I mentioned earlier, and the mother of the little girl over there." Gibran pointed at Warissah who was in the corner of the room. Humeirah and Saabir exchanged a smile.

"Papa, I took your briefcase by mistake," continued Humeirah, "Your leather bag is like mine. I'm sorry, I thought it was mine." She handed it over, eyeing him closely to see if he showed any sign of apprehension or unease.

"Oh," said Gibran, indifferently.

Maybe, she realised, she should have waited to be alone with him; he would have been compelled to drop the mask. Just then, Hashim, another guest, and Humeirah's uncle, walked by and started a conversation with him.

Humeirah turned to Saabir. "I have never seen you before. Most people I come across are usually businessmen, lawyers, or work in the corporate field. It's so rare to come across a writer, especially *here—*"

"Yes," he chortled, "I don't think one would easily find writers in these Memon gatherings."

"Are you—"

"No, I'm not Memon. We'd have known each other otherwise. I'm Surti. Still *acceptable* to the Memons," he added with a wink.

"I don't understand the reason for all the smugness of our lot—"

"I know what you mean but give it time. The world is opening up. With increasing wealth and exposure, the Memons as well as the Surtis will realise how obtuse, sheltered, and insensitive they have been in clinging to ethnocentric and endogamous beliefs and practices. For a long time, they have led insular lives, much more so on this small island, so that they never subjected their mores to any serious questioning."

"You sound very optimistic, Saabir. I just think it will only get more parochial with time."

"I understand why you are of this opinion, Humeirah, but hear me out. I always remind myself that thankfully, there are only so many bigoted Memons and Surtis among the lot who deem themselves to be *superior* to everyone. There's something to be said about how ethnocentric not just the Memons are on our island, but nearly every other community. Do you know that every other Mauritian I meet has a story about how he or she is *not* like the other Hindus or Muslims on the island, but of some noble ancestry of some sort?"

Humeirah chuckled.

"You're right," she said, "but also, you're very intriguing...and refreshingly honest! Please tell me about your books."

"Oh, you know," said Saabir, "I've lost the habit of explaining what I write. No one really asks. So, let's see, I mostly write about human behaviour and philosophy."

"Fiction or nonfiction?"

"Primarily nonfiction."

"And your favourite themes?"

"Well, I think that my writing is influenced by Nietzsche, Lacan and Deleuze. Have you heard of them?"

"Of course! I have their books."

Saabir eyed her with more curiosity than ever. He had rarely come across someone whose attention did not waver at the mention of those names or even his writing. Most people he met usually asked how many books he sold, how much money he made, and whether he would consider writing school books instead, since he could generate more money doing that.

"I've been into poetry lately," Humeirah said. "I love the idea of how so much can be said in a compressed form."

"I have published a book of poetry too," said Saabir, suddenly warmer than he had been.

Humeirah smiled and said: "They say that in Mauritius, we produce the highest number of poets per square metre."

"Really? But again, it's not surprising. Living on an island, being constantly surrounded by the sea hammers the notion of infinity in our beings. Every time we look out, we somehow catch sight of the horizon, and know that it is only an imaginary line that deceives us into thinking that this is the end. This is all there is to it... But of course, we, the rational-minded, know better. Every time we peer at the horizon, we are reminded of Nature's deceit. We wonder what other forms of deceptions exist out there which cloud our thinking. And then the sun, the moon and the clouds do strange things to what we see in the distance. The setting keeps changing, the colours are never the same, and our minds, our hearts are constantly titillated. All this stirs something in us, and a feeling of restlessness settles in our souls forever. It's this very restlessness that is fodder for us poets."

Humeirah smiled again, but differently. She didn't agree with him: the limitedness of the sky was as imaginary as the limitedness of the horizon that he had referred to, so that one didn't have to be on an island to be a poet. But she kept the thought to herself, fearing that the bluntness would upset him. "Tell me about the poems you've written."

"I..." he said but was interrupted by Gibran whose attention was on them for a while, and who seemed annoyed: "I'm sorry, Saabir. Humeirah always does this. I keep telling her not to get into all those airy-fairy topics that never seem to get anyone anywhere." Gibran laughed a fake laugh to cover his embarrassment.

"No, no," insisted Saabir, "I actually enjoy—"

"Come on Saabir," urged Gibran, as he ushered his protégé towards the dining table.

"Let's get you something to eat and tell you about *lepok lontan* in the late forties when Madame Decartier, a midwife from Bell Village, dressed in white from head to toe, would come in a pony-drawn stagecoach to deliver babies at our home in Louis Pasteur Street."

Humeirah stood rooted to the ground as the two moved away from her. Not only had an interesting conversation been cut short, but she had also been belittled in front of a total stranger. It was not the first time. Over the years, she had tried to be indifferent to it, to no avail. She knew her weakness: as her father said, she was oversensitive. But she also knew she was powerless to change. Still, she reminded herself that, next time, she would try to be more numb.

Humeirah searched the room for Warissah and noticed that she was with Ambareen, Haider's younger sister. Humeirah and Ambareen barely talked, but Humeirah enjoyed her company; something was raw, simple, and straightforward about her. One could easily imagine Ambareen entering the bond of matrimony, conforming to the norms and social conventions that she would become acquainted with by observing others and mimicking their behaviour. She would never have a reason to complain about rules and conventions, never feel that they imposed a burden on her, and so, fit nicely into the big puzzle that life was. At twenty-one, Ambareen was waiting for an offer of marriage from a respectable and decent Memon boy, and her parents, Mr. and Mrs. Shah, were waiting for an eligible bachelor to come forward. They had an idea who eventually would, since the community of Memons was small and everyone knew everyone, so that at any given time, one could single out potential suitors based solely on age.

Ambareen's simplicity and childlike manner also made her the ideal companion to Warissah who clung to her throughout the party that day. It also suited those who were relieved of the chore of babysitting her, and reduced the burden on Humeirah as her mother; her carer.

IV

# -Questions with no Answers-

"Man by nature desires not to know." Humeirah

In comfortable leather sofas adjacent to each other, Haider and Saabir sat cross-legged, making polite conversation. Haider was distracted by someone he had been observing from the corner of his eye. Saabir did not interest him—he was just a writer. It was acceptable for a woman to write, to draw, to paint...but a man? A man was meant to work hard, strive to climb the social ladder, make money, and command the respect of his peers.

The lady wore a dainty shalwar khameez of organza. She was Sana. The peacock-blue and ochre sequins in the fabric blended with a pair of peep toe shoes and diamond filigree earrings. Haider noticed everything.

*What a contrast to the woman I married.*

Humeirah was within his field of vision, and he turned his attention to her.

*Look at her lipstick. So bright and red and garish. Looks like what a Calcattia would wear. I bought her an expensive one from a duty-free store in Dubai, and I've never seen her use it. And those shoes! They're so tacky and don't even match her shalwar khameez. She has no style.*

"How long does it take for a book to be published?" Haider said, reverting to Saabir.

"It depends, but I'd say about two to three years by the time it is written, edited, and sent out for printing."

"Hmm," said Haider, still stealing quick glances at Humeirah. There was a strange air about her.

While the thought ran through his mind, the protracted silence between Saabir and him crossed the limits of acceptability. "I was thinking of investing money in the publishing industry," he said. "What are your thoughts on that?"

Haider's eyes remained fixed on his interlocutor, as he feigned to absorb what was said.

*It would be better if she left. She is like a statue. She evokes the same feelings in me. I hate her, I hate her presence, I hate the way she looks, I hate the way she dresses, I hate the way she talks. She is a shame, a shame to me and my family. The worst thing that could happen to a man. Why can't she be like other women?*

The truth was that Haider would not be able to stand it if Humeirah left. It would be an insult to his ego, but he wasn't aware of it. He just knew that he could not divorce her because it would cause a strain between the families, and more importantly, everyone knew everyone in the Memon community. *Ki dimoun pou dir?* What would people say? It could even jeopardise Ambareen's prospects of marrying a good Memon boy.

Earlier, Haider had rushed home after a day's work, showered, and changed into fresh clothes. On an ordinary day, he would have returned at an hour when everyone was asleep and be the first to wake up. Then, Shanthi would prepare breakfast; the only meal he ate regularly at home. Haider worked every day except on Sundays which he spent hanging out with friends and playing golf at the Gymkhana Club in Vacoas. Occasionally, he threw a party at home and invited friends and co-workers.

At his sister's house that day, he was dressed in a muted black shirt that complemented a lighter shade of black trousers, so that his tall and athletic figure stood out. Haider was good-looking and at thirty-five, women detected the confidence he exuded and succumbed easily to his charm.

Saabir had just ended a litany about the publishing industry. Again, there was an awkward silence. To temporise, Haider took a few sips of tea.

"Will you excuse me?" he finally said, placing the cup on the saucer and standing up. "Sure," replied Saabir in relief.

Haider walked over to Humeirah who was sitting in the corner of the room, staring at something he couldn't quite figure out.

"Humeirah? What's going on?"

Humeirah looked up. This man knew her beyond the cloth wrapped around her body, she thought.

*What wasted intimacy.*

At least, that was all. There was solace in knowing that a part of her remained a secret to him, and to the world.

Still, a feeling of intense irritation crept up in her, but she maintained her composure.

"Humeirah, I asked you a question. You like to talk, so talk."

She was taken aback by the tone, the comment, the audacity.

*This man doesn't share anything with me, and yet, demands a right to know what I am thinking.*

She returned a blank expression. This time it was his turn to be annoyed.

*I feel like ripping her apart! The inert vegetable that she is, and scrape her from inside.*

He thought of inciting her to react. "Where did you go last Tuesday?" he asked, at a volume set to display anger but also the desire to be discreet.

"Eh?" he continued, "Shanthi told me you left Warissah behind and went off don't-know-where. You stupid woman."

Humeirah's inert expression did not change.

"You'd better watch out, you hear me? I won't tolerate your nonsense. Vijay won't drive you around if you don't change."

Humeirah watched her husband move away and join in a conversation with his parents and her father.

*Why did people ever get married?*

Haider was right. Throughout that day, Humeirah had been restless, aching to be alone to mull over the letter in the briefcase. She was surprised however, that she had displayed outward signs of agitation, and doubly so that of all persons, her husband had picked them up.

During the party that day, her eyes were often fixed on her father. Here was a tired man who looked older than his age. The grey at his temples, the wrinkles that gave him a haggard appearance, and the crow's feet around his eyes, stood out. She hadn't realised how much he had aged since the time she remembered him as a child and an adolescent. Now, before her was an old man whose watch showed a specific time; its needles stuck on the moment Soraya had said "No".

*What a waste of a man who could have explored the wonders of a world filled with emotions.*

*In him, and in many human beings, emotions are numbed and smothered by the hand of a baker who forces them into identical moulds to turn them into carbon copies of one another.*

*Papa has suffered like me; he too has been deprived of—*

*What exactly has he been deprived of?*

*I can't describe it yet. Perhaps the word will come to me soon.*

*But Papa forced himself to adapt, to fit in. Today he is a devil because he is not himself; just someone who lives to please others. He will die thinking he was admired for following the rules.*

She was consoled by the thought. Then, the little voice re-emerged and cried out: "But why me? Why did you do that to me? You didn't learn from your mistake!"

Humeirah's eyes welled up with tears that she tried to hold back.

*If Papa had my spirit, he would have fought to marry the woman he loved.*

*But we are not born equal; we are born with varying mettle, and once we accept that, it's easier to understand why people behave differently from one another—and easier to be tolerant towards one another.*

*But am I any better? Didn't I allow myself to be forced into this union?*

V

# -The Age of Absurdity-

"Morality is a matter of taste, and everyone has a different aesthetic." Humeirah

One year ago, Warissah went to Clinique Darné to meet her cousin Hannah for the first time, and saw a tiny baby wrapped in a pink flannel shawl.

"Dolly and the baby look alike!" she said.

Shaheen smiled an exhausted half-smile and nodded.

Many months earlier, the day the gynaecologist confirmed the pregnancy, Shaheen dropped by at the supermarket in Phoenix and filled a shopping cart with items from the organic food section. Just to be sure, she selected the most expensive brands. Her husband Zain usually did the shopping—the weekly task assigned to him—but with the news that their first child was on the way, Shaheen felt the need to take over. The baby had to get the best of everything.

Over the next few months, she wished to read everything about the dos and don'ts of pregnancy, childcare and motherhood. By the time Hannah was born, a neat stack of self-help books stood on every kind of table in the house, collecting dust. Still, Shaheen somehow knew exactly what to do, and couldn't wait to put it to action. In the delivery room, when her daughter let out her first cry, she turned to the doctor, tired and sweaty, and said: "Do you know the cry of a newborn baby is called a vagitus?" Then, she added: "But I still don't know how to use it in a sentence."

The doctor and nurses exchanged smiles. "It's the effect of the epidural," he said, and changed his mind when a short while after, she began issuing orders to the nurses in attendance that her baby had to be brought to her as soon as possible to be breastfed. She had read that newborns weaned on formula went on to detest everything else, including breast milk and the much-needed colostrum. The first two weeks are crucial, she explained, since mammary glands produce a thick, sticky fluid which plays a big role in strengthening the baby's immune system. The nurses listened, some detesting the patronising tone, others admiring her for being well-informed.

But in utter indifference to these reactions, Shaheen's mastery of the subject and her understanding of matters beyond the reach of many, reinforced how she felt about herself, and the command she believed she had on life.

In Shaheen's world, pacifiers were also prohibited since she had come across an article in an edition of *Reader's Digest* that condemned its use, claiming that it interfered with the alignment and development of milk teeth.

Everybody agreed that Shaheen was a good mother, but since she had read from reliable as well as unreliable sources, fact fused with fiction so that the world was not so much a museum of discovery than a labyrinth of danger.

Soon, Shaheen also became an authority in the Memon community about matters involving food habits and nutrition. It came about after she began chiding everyone for believing that Extra virgin olive oil had more of everything nutritious than plain olive oil (which was easily assumed since the former was more expensive), and therefore a better substitute. Patiently, she explained how one was more resistant to heat, and could therefore be used for deep frying, while the other was more suitable for salads. In a separate phase, she advised everyone to avoid rice cookers, and to boil rice in extra water and strain it to control blood sugar levels or prevent the onset of diabetes. Suffice it to say that Shaheen's extended commentaries about healthy and unhealthy ingredients, the knowledge she gained during her research, and the jargon she thus acquired and heard herself use, flooded her with a sense of well-being, and gave her one more reason to be.

But Shaheen was opinionated beyond matters related to nutrition and paediatrics. Among many things, she gave a lot of importance to birthdays.

That day, on the occasion of her daughter's birthday, children and adults, in clusters that qualified their interests, were dispersed across the sitting room. A cluster of older boys was engrossed in dismantling a toy car while another, consisting of younger ones, was engrossed in a treasure hunt. Seated on the carpet in the sitting room, Warissah and four other girls were exchanging stories about their dolls as well as trying to blow up the balloons that Hannah's grandparents had brought.

Earlier, Shaheen had gotten into an argument with Zain because he had wanted to decorate the house with balloons. "For the party," he had said, "for the children."

"Definitely not! It would look so tacky, so unclassy," she retorted, and when he tried to convince her, she burst into tears. Zain gave in. Later, when her parents walked in with a gift for Hannah and a packet of balloons for the children, Shaheen and Zain had exchanged a look and she had shrugged.

Now the single candle that stood on the birthday cake was lit and everyone was asked to gather around the table. By then, Baby Hannah was cranky and restless, so that Shaheen hoped that the cake-cutting and photo-taking sessions would be over soon. Hannah usually took a nap in the afternoon. In a firm embrace, Shaheen held her daughter, and took in the mess in the sitting room.

*What could I do? A birthday party without people wouldn't make sense. I want my daughter to look back and think that she was always special.*

Her attention turned to the noisy chatter of the children, and the occasional high tones of the adults present.

*Hannah will never grow up to be so noisy. I will make sure she is taught good manners.*

Hannah's sniffles then turned into wailing. Shaheen hastened to give the cue for the birthday song, and on hearing it, Hannah calmed down and looked around curiously. The children joined in the singing, incoherent and out of tune. How Shaheen wished she had asked them to practise it beforehand!

Baby Hannah was too young to blow out the candle on the cake, so the children begged Shaheen to be given the chance. "Me!" said a little boy; "Me!" shouted another; "Me!" pleaded a girl, the shortest of the lot, as she raised her arm and stretched it as high as she could. The room resounded with different voices, each tinged with a unique quality that the competitor had concocted in an urgent act of creativity.

At that age, children didn't know about the science of probability which would later compel many in similar scenarios to give up and stop trying; the day many would realise the universal law, that in any given situation, only a few would make it.

"Let Warissah do it," said Shaheen suddenly. "She is Hannah's cousin."

Warissah could feel everyone's eyes on her, and couldn't stop beaming. So far, her birthday had been celebrated once—when she was three. She could recall the pink and light green napolitaines and samosas that Shanthi had prepared on the occasion, which she had gone on to place around the homemade cake.

When it was time to blow out the candle on the cake, Humeirah had helped Warissah climb a chair, and together, she and Shanthi had held her while she had leaned over. Warissah recalled that there weren't many people at the birthday—not as many as at this one; in fact, she was almost certain that there was no one other than the three of them and Vijay.

Now, in apprehension and excitement, Warissah moved closer to the cake.

"No, wait," Shaheen said. "It might be too dangerous. Let me do it."

Warissah's heart sank.

She watched Shaheen blow out the candle, turn to Hannah who was in her arms, smile and kiss her, and pose for a photo before Zain.

Since Hannah was too young to eat cake, Shaheen cut a thin slice and feigned feeding her, urging Zain to hurry up. The children were asked to clap, more photos were taken, and the cake was finally distributed among those present.

Finally, Hannah was led away to her bedroom. While singing to her, Shaheen's mind wandered to a thought that now troubled her. What if, one day, her daughter, by then older and more autonomous, saw the photo of her being fed cake? Would she blame her?

Shaheen waited for Hannah to fall asleep and stepped out of the room. She went up to Zain and shared her concern. Attentively, he listened, then looked at her, sighed discreetly, picked up the camera and deleted the photos. She beamed, but caught up in the moment, failed to notice how perturbed he looked.

Zain realised that day that he had been so engrossed in capturing every moment of his daughter's birthday that he had merely witnessed it through the screen of his camera.

VI

## -Absence and Presence-

"Old is gold... Or Time, that conniving creature: had it entered into a secret covenant with Imagination, and sought to blot out bad memories and embellish good ones further?" The loud voice in Humeirah's head

The guests were on the patio helping themselves to the snacks and confectioneries laid out on a long banquet table hired for the occasion, showering Shaheen with praise for the meticulous choice of food and decor. At that moment, it was everything she wished for.

Haider remained seated throughout the afternoon, even when everyone stood up and approached the table for the cake-cutting ceremony. Shaheen, his favourite sister and younger to him by two years, had just served him a plate of sweetmeats, and was now in the kitchen making him a cup of tea.

Haider often complained that he wished she had found a better match than her husband Zain who had relegated her to living in Beau Bassin. Time and again he also reminded her of her missed opportunity with Parvez, a first cousin, who had sought her hand in marriage at about the same time as Zain, but who she had turned down, saying: *li pa al dan mwa.*

"What does it mean to say someone doesn't suit you?" Haider had then pestered. "Parvez is on my team, and he moves around with us. He will look after you well. And if you marry him, you'll be next door to Mum and Dad."

The matter was decided when Parvez withdrew the offer, sensing Shaheen's reluctance, and wishing by every means to eschew the embarrassment. Soon after, following assiduous efforts of his mother to get in touch with distant relatives in Karachi, he was wedded to a simple and undifficult Memon from there.

At the house in Beau Bassin that day, Haider was discussing—what everyone called *politics*—with Arif, a cousin, who had taken over from Saabir, who in turn, had moved away to get food. A minister had been caught in a compromising situation with a sex worker and the news had gone viral. Not far away, Gibran was in a tête-à-tête with Zain, talking over him, complaining about prices and comparing them to when he was a young boy: "Look at the prices of eggs: sixty rupees a dozen. When I was a small boy, in the fifties, I remember it cost only sixty cents. Did you look at the price of butter? They just raised the prices. Again, sixty rupees when it was only three rupees then. And sugar. We produce sugar in Mauritius and yet it now costs fifty-one rupees." Zain lowered his eyes, nodding every now and then. "I am worried about what's in store for my granddaughter and the generations that will follow," Gibran continued. "Everything will only get worse. This is a sign of Qayamat." Gibran's words echoed those of his parents when he was a young boy, overhearing them voice the same concern. In turn, theirs had been an echo of their own parents', both at a comparable age and social event.

Haider walked up to his father-in-law who smiled and patted him on the shoulder, not condescendingly, but with a touch of humility and respect. To an outsider, Gibran seemed to treat his son-in-law like a father would a son who had outperformed him. Gibran, however, thought that his gesture made Haider look up to him as a fatherly figure, while the latter interpreted it as a sign of servility and weakness.

The conversation carried on. Individuals hopped from one group to another, one cluster to another, catching up with the latest, filling their minds with enough to discuss about then, and in the aftermath, all vital for the upkeep of the flow of life. Gossip, however petty and detrimental to individual autonomy, and no matter how widely deplored and condemned, policed society and upheld its mores more robustly than any other mechanism in place.

Humeirah was in a corner, eating and observing everything from afar. Her daughter was seated at one of the child-size plastic tables Shaheen had bought for the occasion.

Surrounded by other children, with one hand resting on Dolly, Warissah was helping herself to the pastry with the other. At one point, unsure of how soft the mini banana tart was, she bit into it with more energy than she should have, so that the remainder crumbled all over her dress and on the floor. The children laughed. Warissah dusted herself and leaned over to collect the crumbs in a paper napkin, but when she straightened up, most of it still lay on the ground.

Humeirah wondered how her daughter, once lacking autonomy, had now picked up those moves. It could only be through the influence of people around her. But who were they? Shanthi? Her classmates? Ambareen? Was there someone else she didn't know about? Maybe Vijay?

Her attention went to the pink dress Warissah was wearing, and how she couldn't recall seeing it before. Shanthi had probably picked it before leaving for the weekend; maybe a gift from Haider's parents after their most recent trip to Paris.

Haider's parents hardly spent time in the country. On their return, however, they never failed to shower their granddaughters, Warissah and Hannah, with gifts of shoes, dresses and the latest doll collections. On Shanthi's advice, Warissah abstained from removing the dolls from their packaging, let alone play with them. The one time she did, Shanthi insisted that she keep the plastic wrapper intact, and Warissah hadn't enjoyed the experience. Now, whenever Warissah received a doll, she put it away in a drawer of her wardrobe, supposedly for the children she would have one day, as Shanthi had advised.

Mr. and Mrs. Shah spoiled both their granddaughters, Warissah and Hannah. When Haider, Shaheen and Ambareen were adolescents, they would leave them in the care of maids who lived in the quarters attached to their house, and go away on holiday. They said that their children were old enough to take care of themselves; that there was only so much they could do because there was no *bharosa* in life, and that anything could suddenly happen, so that they had to enjoy themselves while they could, adding that they also wished to make the most of their wealth. "Otherwise, what's the point of all the toil?" said Mr. Shah, who early in his career, had launched a furniture franchise across the island, invested some of the returns on the stock market, only to retire early and leave the business in the hands of his son.

When Mrs. Shah returned from her travels with gifts and curios for everyone, for fun, she threw Tupperware parties at her house. Her initial aspirations were democratic: she wanted to invite everyone, regardless of their financial backgrounds, but soon enough, she and those closest to her noticed how people flocked to her house purely for food and entertainment, and refrained from buying what was on sale and exhibition. Soon enough, her guest list grew shorter and the people left on it were those from the most well-to-do backgrounds.

It was no wonder that word went around that these were merely get-togethers for the snobs of the Memon community, and on hearing about it, Mrs. Shah was offended, but secretly, also a bit proud.

There were consequences to Mr. and Mrs. Shah's attitudes to life.

Shaheen was bitter about her upbringing, and lamented a neglected childhood to them, adding that she didn't want her daughter to suffer as she had done. Perplexed by these outcries, Mr. and Mrs. Shah thought the best way forward was to say nothing.

Lately, however, they were worried about Ambareen—the youngest—known to rely on her brother and sister for everything. They could only hope that the Memon boy she married would look after her, and concluded that to do so, he would have to be wealthy. Otherwise, like what Anjum, one of Mr. Shah's brothers, did to his daughter Samia, they would have to marry Ambareen off to a Calcattia. The problem with Samia was that she was already twenty-eight and had not received proposals from Memons. By thirty, the eligible men in her age group would be married, and she would be doomed to remain a spinster. In the most well-meaning, as well as distraught and candid tone, Samia's mother Shahista, told everyone, including her own daughter, that the reason was that she was not fair, lean and beautiful like most Memon girls—a fact, plain and simple. As a result, not even the few with the required mettle to tell Shahista off for making the statement, did so.

While Mr. and Mrs. Shah were anxious about the future of their daughter, they derived solace from Haider, their only son, who had followed in his father's footsteps. Still, undeniably, his wife Humeirah was a concern. She was just not right for him. Early in their marriage, the two had started sleeping in separate rooms—clearly a bad sign. What perturbed them even more, was Haider's relationship with Warissah since he was distant from her. When friends hinted that it was connected to his neglected childhood, the Shahs denied it. After all, hadn't their daughter Shaheen turned out to be a good mother?

Haider overheard the gossip but dismissed it without saying much; it had nothing to do with his childhood. The truth was that learning that he would father a girl had not been the most exciting news, especially since he wouldn't want another child—at least not with Humeirah.

Haider was a man of the world. On weekends, at Caudan Waterfront, in the company of friends, he tried to secure the best deals, expanding his network, connecting with the powerful, and enjoying the privileges that came with it. He wanted to be known by everyone, lend a helping hand to those who mattered, solving their problems, and letting them solve his. He had toiled hard to get far in life and wanted it to mean something.

During those outings, by the time everyone would have bullied everyone else into ignoring calls from mothers and wives, mocked them for answering their phones, or hooted at any hint of submissiveness in their tone thereafter, it would be late in the night. Haider would then settle the bill, aware that everything in life involved a give-and-take.

"I am leaving," said Humeirah to Haider who was surrounded by friends at the birthday party. By then, most of the guests had left.

"Are you coming?" she asked, unaware of how loud of a tone it was.

Haider was annoyed. Now, he would have to think of an excuse that would sound polite and reasonable to everyone.

*Fucking bitch.*

"No, go ahead. I want to stay back and talk to Arif about something," he said.

"Do you want me to send Vijay to pick you up after he drops me off?"

Haider paused.

"No. I'll ask Arif for a lift. Go home. Vijay is waiting."

Haider's excuse to stay back was not new: he rarely went home with Humeirah after family outings.

But what she wasn't aware of that day, was that he was eager to get rid of her so that he could meet the lady he had laid his eyes on.

# VII

## -The Use and Abuse of Hope-

"What goes around, doesn't come around—*You* make it come around." Humeirah

It was usual for Warissah to spend the night with her paternal grandparents, especially on weekends when Ambareen could take care of her. Not that Ambareen couldn't on other days, but she wished to have the time to herself, watching her favourite TV shows, and calling friends. She didn't have a child, a husband, a job, or responsibilities that forced her to stick to a routine, so that to fill the lacuna, she wanted to seem busy at the time other women she looked up to, were. In any case, she told herself it would be training for when she would inevitably be a wife and mother.

Warissah had spare clothes in Gibran's house too—the other place where she liked to spend the night. Almost every weekend she was given a choice, and that night, Warissah asked to stay at her aunt's.

That was why, after the party at Shaheen's house, Haider and Warissah stayed back and Humeirah was the only passenger in the car. After passing Phoenix, Vijay took a different route to Floreal because of the traffic, and followed the road to the airport, passing by the market in Vacoas. After that, they went through a series of small alleys before driving past Clinique Darné. Only he knew that route—Humeirah's least favourite, because the roads and houses were clumped together so that the sharp turns gave her motion sickness and made her claustrophobic.

Earlier, along the M1, the car had slowed down because of the traffic. Humeirah had peered at the violet-indigo, light green and dark green leaves of the tall and sturdy trees by the roadside whose names she didn't know. Gusts of wind kept tugging at the branches, depriving them of some of the leaves—the weakest. The weather was deteriorating; the sky darkening. The weather station had issued a cyclone warning Class 1.

Humeirah had mulled over the unnatural course of things: how the leaves, prematurely detached from their source of sustenance, became playthings to greater forces, and were carried away to inconspicuous places to rot, when they could have rotted much later. Amid the ravaging scenery of leaves resisting and leaves getting detached, she noticed a bird's nest tumbling out from a mango tree—an image that would remain etched in her mind's eye. Later, she would remember how the eggs had dropped out faster than the nest.

Her thoughts were interrupted by Vijay's sniffles.

"Vijay, is everything all right?"

The concern prompted him to burst out into loud sobs.

"Madame, she lost it. I went home just now, and she said—"

"What? Who...are you talking about?"

"Anjili, Madame," he replied, "she lost the baby."

"I'm so sorry, Vijay. How is she now?"

"She is crying, Madame, but she's OK. She said so."

"Did you call the doctor?"

"Yes, I must take her to the hospital. The doctor said that he has to do a check-up and clean something inside."

"OK, at least she is not in danger. Don't worry."

There was a pause. "But I feel guilty, Madame," he said in a small voice. "I think all this wouldn't have happened if—"

"Why do you say that?"

"I haven't been a good man! I brought it upon myself."

Vijay burst into louder sobs.

Humeirah remembered the extra-marital affair. "Whatever it is that you have done wrong, Vijay, the loss of the baby has nothing to do with it."

"No, Madame," he insisted, "Swamiji gave a talk on the radio about Karma. He said that when you do bad things, somehow you pay for it one day. It makes so much sense. It's because of my misdeeds that I am suffering now."

Humeirah shook her head: "It has nothing to do with that."

"No, Madame. You don't understand...I've done something terrible related to...related to my marriage."

"I think I know what you are alluding to, but trust me, don't blame yourself."

Humeirah wondered whether it was worth explaining her thoughts. "Give it a try," said the little voice.

"You see, Vijay, bad things happen to everyone. Most of the time, there is no reason behind them. Look at it as something we can't explain and have no control over, like winning the lottery or being born in a certain place and time, which are all purely brought about through luck, nothing else. They have nothing to do with whether you worked for them to happen, or for that matter, *deserved* them. In the end, nothing differentiates the so-called fortunate one from the one bearing the misfortune. Isn't it sad and unfair?

But that's life. The truth is that when bad things happen, people can't bear the pain and sadness that come with it, so they come up with reasons to justify it. For instance, they say that it's the devil who did it, and resort to prayer as a result. Or that God has a reason for what He did, and that in the long run, the reason will become clear. Or, exactly in the manner you said, that it's because they did something wrong that they're now paying for it. All these are nothing but *coping mechanisms*."

Humeirah took a deep breath.

"It's so easy to blame something bad that's happened on your past deeds," she continued. "You are only trying to find an *excuse* for what happened. Don't blame yourself. What happened to Anjili is sad and unjust, yes, but it has nothing to do with you and your actions. The truth is that for everything bad that happens to us, we will always be able to scour our past and find something or the other to feel guilty about, and blame. It's pointless."

Vijay remained silent. He had tried to follow Humeirah's explanation, but it was in the tone of her voice that he had found comfort. "You are right, Madame. It's because I did something wrong that my wife is paying for it."

Humeirah let out a quiet sigh.

*Maybe it's good that Vijay is blaming himself. At least he'll be loyal to Anjili from now on. And maybe it will make it easier for him to come to terms with the cruelty and injustice of what happened.*

*Maybe that's the whole point of coping mechanisms. They provide explanations to us, we who hunger for them, when in truth, there are none. And what we get in turn is solace from the harsh reality of rampant injustice.*

Humeirah's thoughts went to the bird that had lost its nest and eggs.

*I don't know much about animals, but I know the bird won't look for reasons to justify what happened.*

*Yes, maybe the bird will show signs of distress, but it will build another nest and lay fresh eggs.*

*And who knows? Maybe be robbed of them again.*

Humeirah remembered the words she had read while passing by a banner at a protest march near Les Jardins de la Compagnie in Port Louis: *"Pas d'excuse pour la cruauté! Pas d'excuse pour la violence!"*— "There's no excuse for cruelty! No excuse for violence!"

They meant something different to her now.

# VIII

## -The Evil of Monotony-

"God too grew tired of monotony and brought in the serpent." Humeirah

The car came to a stop in the driveway. Vijay was deep in thought, wondering how he could mend his ways. The toughest was to convince Hanisha that he didn't want to see her again. How would she react? Would she resist? On top of that, she was right next door. How would he manage to avoid her? The other maids in the house were growingly irascible about her stepping out to see her lover—Hanisha said they couldn't stand her being happy.

Maybe he could use that as an excuse to tell her they should stop meeting.

Vijay watched Humeirah enter the house, and when she turned around to look at him, he nodded and drove away in the direction of Belle Rose. Humeirah locked the front door.

The house was quieter than usual. Shanthi was in Eau Coulée for the weekend. Her only son Raj, a stout thirty-year-old, a *teknisyen*, earned a living by doing odd jobs. The sudden death of her husband, a taxi driver, when their son was only fifteen, had left both without a regular income. The meagre savings the sole breadwinner had left behind were enough to get by for only two months. Raj had insisted on quitting school—he didn't learn much anyway and said he could be more productive on his own.

In a short time, he picked up a range of skills by observing his mentors; a few men working on a housing project near his house. Two months later, Raj was already moving from house to house, fixing simple glitches with the wiring, mending water pipes, or replacing bulbs that were difficult to reach. But sometimes he had no work, and it was tougher to secure any as he was getting older. Now that he had a family—his wife Deepa and their children, Anusha and Valesha—he was dependent on Shanthi who held back just enough to cover transport on weekends and handed him the rest of her salary.

Humeirah's fingers glided over the bannister that felt unusually cold as she trudged up the stairs to her bedroom.

*Matter becomes cold when it loses energy. But it depends on the substance: metals lose heat faster than non-metals.*

Her stomach groaned—she had barely eaten at the party, but Shanthi never failed to leave cooked food in the fridge before her weekly break. Before getting to it, however, she had to change into something comfortable.

The hollowness in her stomach was overpowering. She slipped out of her shalwar khameez and hung it on the wooden rack. The dress, once stainless, once creaseless, was now intertwined with memories. She found it hard to concentrate.

*People are obsessed with the idea of relieving the most minor discomfort, the most minor pain. What's wrong with pain? Pain evokes sadness, breeds anger. Aren't they as legitimate as every other feeling or emotion?*

*Isn't it easier to put up with the torture of hunger than the torture of the thoughts I have?*

*No. The torture of hunger is as unbearable as any other.*

*We are always trying to get rid of pain—no. We are always trying to get rid of happiness too. Even Candide got tired of the absolute bliss of Eldorado.*

*Surely, it's not pleasure or pain that's man's enemy, but the monotony of the same experience.*

Humeirah took a quick shower, changed into a white nightie, and went downstairs to a kitchen that was neat and clean. When she opened the fridge, her eyes fell on plastic containers placed on top of one another. One contained plain rice, a second, dal, a third, fried pieces of chicken. She scooped some rice out with a ladle, used it to transfer some dal, and picked a few pieces of chicken. Shanthi would have required a separate spoon for every dish—a rule didn't make sense to Humeirah since rice was dry anyway, and all she had to do was to make sure it didn't stick to the ladle when she dished out the dal. She heated the food in the microwave and took the plate upstairs, relieved that Shanthi wasn't there to tell her off.

*People seem to be obsessed with the idea of cleanliness.*

*The sign of outward dirt indicates inward corruption... People make such strange associations. If I spill the food, well, so what? I'll just clean it.*

In her bedroom, Humeirah went up to the bookshelf and rummaged through the CD wallet that stood on one of the shelves. She played a few songs she had known in her schooldays.

One of them evoked the memory of her on the school bus, travelling along the Grand River North West bridge on entering Port Louis. She remembered how different the view was compared to when she would look out from a car. From the bus, it was the river, the bushy trees around it, the view of the ancient unfinished tower from the colonial days. From the car, it was the railings of the bridge, the vehicles ahead and those in the opposite lane.

Then, Humeirah wondered how connections were made; how memories were evoked. She played a few more songs, wishing to figure out what feelings and memories each stirred.

After a while, the songs conveyed nothing, but she kept at it, switching them for new ones, craving what she had been privy to, moments earlier.

Still nothing.

Oblivious to the time spent in search of a feeling, and out of defeat in fighting monotony, an exhausted Humeirah crawled into bed.

IX

## -A Good Memon Boy-

"It's not money, status, or power that creates inequalities, but emotions." The little voice in Humeirah's head

Kareem was related to Humeirah because he was her cousin—her late mother's brother's son. At twenty-two he had just graduated with a bachelor's degree in Business Management from a university in the UK.

In his school days, Kareem had skipped most classes, believing that his main objective was to make money, and conventional education could not teach him that. On days that his friends would be boarding the school bus, he would be accompanying his father Hashim to Louis Pasteur Street where he owned a shop selling gardening paraphernalia, assisting him in running it till five. Kareem barely managed to scrape through his A-level exams, but it did not bother him. He aspired to rise in status among the Memons because his father wasn't as wealthy as most of them.

Kareem believed that he was a simple boy who wanted to marry a simple girl, start a family, make money, and die a good death. He wasn't asking for much was the message he was conveying, and everyone commended him for his humility.

At home, he watched Bollywood movies, surfed the internet to look for pornography, drank soda and ordered fast food almost daily. At the core, he was really a homebody, and this helped him assert himself vis-à-vis those who went clubbing, drank alcohol and had fun with girls. He was different; he was a good Memon boy. Deep down, his heart swelled at that thought, and made him feel he deserved the best.

In no time, from the slim and tall boy he once was, no longer could he tuck his shirt, and as it stretched over his stomach, the last three or four buttons seemed as if they were about to pop. When he moved away, his friends opened their eyes wide and whispered: "Ena krim ek Kareem"—There is crime with Kareem, it being suggested that the buttons posed a threat to passers-by. Although many believed that, by itself, the statement lacked humour, everyone was amused by the tone in which it was said, and of course, the assonance and alliteration therein, and sensing what was expected of them, joined in the collective merriment, so that before long, nearly all the members of the Memon community knew that there is crime with Kareem, except for Kareem himself.

Because Kareem eventually had differences with his father Hashim, he decided to start his own business selling baby products to merchants who owned shops in Port Louis. When it flourished, his relatives took to mentioning the next step expected of him: getting married. While some just teased and asked when the Big Day would be, others advised that it was better to settle down early, without explaining the logic. Kareem smiled, nodded, but deep down was worried that he would die alone and single without children and grandchildren to fill the void.

The problem was that there weren't many Memon girls of his age: Safina, his first cousin, was slightly cross-eyed, and Anaaya, his second cousin, was taller than him—*ki dimoun pou dir?*

What would people say? His parents' generation, he said, half-jokingly, hadn't done enough, and one day, if he met The One, he would do better and have the maximum number of children deemed acceptable by his generation: four.

A fan of Bollywood, Kareem quickly superimposed the image of Aishwarya Rai, his favourite actress, onto the face of his would-be wife who hovered in the realm of his imagination. But although she had to be as alluring, he said she also had to be the *homely type.*

"After the first seven years, disaster always strikes in a marriage and that's when the test really starts," he would say, whenever he wanted to share his insight on the subject. "It's important for the guy to have a beautiful wife so that in times of trouble, when he can't stand her, he will still be able to love her and put up with it. It's the only way for a marriage to survive." He also said that the recipe for a successful marriage was that his wife shouldn't work for any other than him: Kareem believed that respectable Memon girls either worked for their husbands or became housewives.

Ambareen, he was told, was a good Memon girl who would tend to his needs and give in to the condition. There was only one problem: he had observed her closely at a few family events, and her nose was a bit crooked, her breasts not very big, and she didn't have the glamorous look of most Memon girls.

"You can't get any other good girl," said his mother Fatima. "At least she's not like those other cheap Memon girls who have boyfriends, drink, and go to clubs. You can rest assured that she hasn't been around." Kareem was still not convinced. "Humeirah's...mad," someone had said. "Just be careful. It must be in the family. Maybe Ambareen is mad too." Others had confirmed it.

Ambareen was neither directly nor closely related to Humeirah; she was her sister-in-law because of Humeirah's marriage with Haider. In their ignorance, it had completely slipped their minds that genes didn't cross over sideways but were only passed on downwards. More importantly, they had forgotten that Humeirah was Kareem's first cousin, and if anyone was more likely to share the same gene as her, it was Kareem, not Ambareen.

After having the conversation with his mother, Kareem asked Ustaad Ashraf if he could help him make up his mind. Ustaad Ashraf handed him a piece of paper scribbled in his own hand with Arabic verses. "This is a special prayer called Salaat-ul-Istikhara. Pray two rakat nafl before you go to bed, read this dua and Allah will guide you, Insha Allah."

That night, after following the instructions, Kareem had a dream where a voice called out from afar: "The grass is green." The image of a pasture flashed before his eyes. Ustaad Ashraf said it was a good dream and could only have come from Allah: "Green and white are good colours. If you dreamt of something red or black it would have meant that the match was not good." That day, Kareem gave his mother Fatima the green light and said that he was interested to meet Ambareen and accept her as his future wife. Fatima was relieved at the prospect of having a son who would soon be married.

Still, as time went by, Kareem began to harbour doubts. Ambareen was nowhere close to Aishwarya Rai. He tried to recall the dream he had had that night after the special prayer, figuring out if there were patches of red or black—maybe a red rose or a black stone—forgotten in the lush green grass. Unfortunately, there was none—the field had been quite green.

Fatima tried to persuade him to get over his doubts. "We'll have to go and look for a Memon girl for you in India. Do you want that?"

Kareem dreaded the thought. The girls from there were pretty and homely, but also conservative. How would they get along? And if she was lacking in refinement, he would be teased for having found a *cabri dan len*. There was also the risk of adjustment problems—the widely acknowledged suffering of Memon women of the previous generation who had migrated from India and Pakistan to marry local Memon men.

Then, one morning, Kareem woke up from a deep sleep and everything made sense. Ambareen hadn't been around—that was what mattered. That's how a good Memon boy would and should think, he told himself.

"Finally! Our youngest will be married!" exclaimed Mr. Shah when Kareem sent the proposal. "Traka fini—we can stop worrying. Our duty is done."

Shaheen was upset. Who were they to speak about any *duty*?

But she soon forgot about that and was distracted by more important matters. She had to draw up a list of the chores in preparation for the wedding and would have to delegate the work to the people she knew. She also had to get a dress for Hannah since it would be the very first wedding she would be attending, and reminded Zain to get ready with the camera.

Shaheen wanted to be the first to break the news to Humeirah. She wanted to know about Kareem, what he liked, what he disliked, and Humeirah surely knew all that.

"You see, we have to give a reply soon," said Shaheen to Humeirah. "What do you think?"

It was Monday, one week after Hannah's birthday, and Shaheen was at Humeirah's house in Floreal.

"Why are you in a hurry to give an answer? Take your time."

"Well, this is an informal proposal. They will only send the formal proposal once they are sure we will say yes. I'm trying to gather as much information as possible about him."

"Why is it so complicated?"

"Well, you know how it works. The boy doesn't want to be embarrassed in case the girl says no, so to play safe, they send the informal proposal first and only when they are sure we will agree, they get an elder family member to come with the formal proposal. So, what do you think of him?"

"He is a first cousin but I don't know him very well," Humeirah said. "Ambareen should decide. Doesn't she want to go to university?"

"What's the point of studying? Let her do it at the University of Mauritius. Anyway, where will her studies take her? She went to college and did her A-levels. She is not very bright anyway. We just want a simple life for her. Kareem is doing well in his business. Maybe she can help him with it. Look at all those decent Memon ladies who help their husbands in their shops. So devoted. In fact, it's better when a woman takes over the business: she can keep a closer eye on her husband."

Shaheen, quiet for a while, resumed. "I think this is a very good match for Ambareen. We were expecting it anyway. It was going to be him, Jawad, or Shahnawaz."

"Have you spoken to her?" asked Humeirah.

"Yes, I mentioned it. She is very excited. She says he is very good looking and is thrilled about getting married. They call each other all the time and stay on the phone for hours—although Fatima doesn't approve of it and says it will bring bad luck. Do you remember the tarts and muffins I ordered for Hannah's birthday? They were from Fatima. I did it on purpose. I wanted to speak to Fatima and get to know her better. She's so sweet, isn't she? She made the cakes and didn't charge a cent. Such decent folk."

Humeirah looked at Shaheen.

*Of course Fatima didn't ask for money.*

Shaheen was still deep in thought.

"I think we should hurry up and accept the proposal," she said. "I heard that Fatima's husband Hashim doesn't deem it necessary for Memons to marry Memons. One of my friends—a Surti—was at their house one day and asked if the akhni they were serving was a Memon dish. Apparently, Fatima's husband gestured to be quiet, saying that the word should never be mentioned."

"You mean, the term 'Memon'?"

"Yes. He believes that we are first and foremost Muslims, and that all other divisions don't count. Although it's a bit hypocritical of him to say that since he doesn't frequent certain mosques because he says Wahabis—*Tablighis*—go there, not the Sunnat Jamaat."

Haider appeared before them. He had just got back from work. "Haider, what do you think of the proposal?" asked Shaheen.

"What proposal?"

"Didn't Mummy and Daddy tell you about it?"

"Yes, yes. Who is Kareem again?"

"Kareem is Humeirah's mamoo's son."

Haider moved his fingers, figuring out the connection. "Oh... you mean Mamoo Hashim's son? Yes, *mais bien sûr*! I remember. I see him at the Jummah Masjid during Friday prayer. A good Memon boy."

Humeirah smirked.

*First, there is the concept of bon fami—a good family; the label given to people based on where they live, how much money they make, whose descendants they are, regardless of the damaged individuals therein who go on to birth and raise children; regardless of the damaged children produced out of these unions, guilty of callousness, mischief, and other evil, and therefore, bad potential partners to others, so that in the end, the label itself means nothing, absolutely nothing. But people still cling to it and use it loosely.*

A good family, thought Humeirah, should have been one where parents weren't damaged, whether by past or existing relationships, so that their children were brought up in a healthy environment. And since that is so rare an occurrence, then at the very least, where the children, through luck or resilience or both, despite everything, got away, unscathed.

Then, Humeirah thought, there is the concept of The Good Memon Boy.

*That's what* They *had said about Haider when I learned about the proposal.*

*How did* They *assess what was good and what was bad? When a guy shed his reserve, nodded, and smiled in a friendly way? When he was occasionally spotted at Friday prayer in the masjid? When despite the years he spent sleeping around with women during his university days abroad, he came back and used some of his charm to show that he had changed?*

"What do you mean by a good Memon boy?" asked Humeirah, directing her attention to Haider, rather than Shaheen. "Every boy is a good Memon boy. Not once have I heard someone say that a Memon boy wasn't good. Aren't there other important questions that you should consider?"

"No," said Haider. "I have seen him in the masjid on Fridays. His father is a good person. I am sure that Kareem is a good person too. He always shows respect for me and says salaam. Very humble boy. Very down-to-earth. I approve."

"Fine. I just don't understand what you mean by good—"

"Good! What more do you want?" Haider turned to Shaheen: "Do you see what I mean? Isn't she fucking annoying?"

"Haider..." called out Shaheen, watching him storm out of the room. "Hah..." she continued, "You've annoyed him again. Anyway, Humeirah, I have to go. Hannah is with the babysitter. I don't like leaving her alone with those people. The next thing you know, my daughter will be rubbing her nose like them—those Calcattias."

# PART III

# The Wedding

# I

## -The Wedding Ceremony-

"What *They* really want is to be in power—because they lack it." The little voice in Humeirah's head

"Arif just called and said that he can arrange to book Rabita Hall," said Faraaz Shah to his son Haider as he sat in the sitting room, surrounded by friends and relatives.

"Rabita Hall? No way!"

"Haider is right," said Yusuf, Mr. Shah's brother, "Nowadays Calcattias celebrate weddings there."

"Yes, the place is shabby, and I don't like the wash basins there," added Afroze Shah, Haider's mother.

Faraaz Shah asked: "What about the Gymkhana Club in Port Louis?"

"It's all right," replied Haider's cousin Suhail, "but the place is going out of fashion."

Haider then added: "I'd rather have it in Domaine Les Pailles or a nice five-star hotel."

***

It is during a wedding ceremony that the underlying tensions within a community emerge: the problem-solving, leadership and managerial skills of volunteer-organisers are put to test; the divergence of opinions and clashes in values reach their peak; rituals are either lauded or criticised. Everyone wants to have a say in the choice of wedding cards, lighting, music, clothes. When a suggestion is shunned, the one who gave it takes offence and pounces on the opportunity to find fault in the tastes and preferences of the other. The dynamics of who-loves-who, who-hates-who, who-kowtows-to-who are unveiled, so that relationships are often altered in the aftermath, some reinforced, others weakened.

When Humeirah and Haider's wedding date was announced, everybody wanted to be around them and have a hand in the most important as well as the most trivial activities. Zeba, who happened to be both Haider and Humeirah's first cousin, and would eventually be their neighbour, drove long distances to order flowers for the Mehendi ceremony and wedding dinner; Shaheen arranged and rearranged the plan for the decor after going through books and magazines; Mrs. Shah observed everything from afar and was flustered over the proposed colour of the wedding cake icing, and criticised most tastes and preferences for being plain or tacky; Mr. Shah ordered samples of invitation cards from the most obscure places, overnight an expert, and when Humeirah voiced the slightest concerns about the preparations—the wedding dress not being delivered on time, or the make-up artist forcing preferences on her—Gibran appeared out of nowhere, and took it upon himself to rectify the matter. Never had so much attention been conferred on her.

During the last week before the wedding ceremony, everyone flocked to Mr. and Mrs. Shah as well as Gibran's house to reel in the liveliness and atmosphere of merriment. In turn, Gibran grew warmer towards Humeirah, overnight attentive to her cares and concerns, asking if she had had lunch or needed his help with anything.

Humeirah wasn't sure if it was for the show since people were always around. She dismissed the thought since her father came up to her to ask the question even when she was alone. Maybe he knew that she was about to leave and be part of a different household—she wasn't sure. Still, she did wonder whether the attention Gibran directed at her would be permanent.

Meanwhile, a few ladies took the liberty to enter Humeirah's bedroom to give her last-minute advice: "Humeirah, this will be a new stage in your life," her aunt Zareen said, "remember it won't be easy. You will have to make many adjustments. A woman's life is never easy." This would be followed by an attempt to educate Humeirah about conjugal life: "When I married Zakir, I thought it would be like a Cinderella story. But it was worse: he sulked so much in the beginning, and I used to cry every day. I didn't know what was wrong, and I was so depressed. I kept going back to my mother and father on the weekends and sometimes, almost every day. One day they told me, 'Zareen, now you must take responsibility for your decision and your life. You can't keep coming to us to soothe you.' I felt very hurt, but now I see that like all parents, they knew what was good for me. I weathered the storm bravely, and after fifteen years, thank God, I can say my husband has changed. He notices when I am not feeling well or when I am too tired. He doesn't do anything about it but, Alhamdulillah, at least he asks. I still have hope, InshaAllah, that he will change even more. I read darood shareef three hundred times every morning after tahajjud, as advised by Ustaad Ashraf."

Another said: "Take care of Haider, Humeirah. Don't let him out of your sight. Don't do what I did. I neglected my duties, and my husband went off to other women—something I regret so much." As the lady sat at the edge of the bed shaking her head, it seemed as if she had come to meet Humeirah not so much as to congratulate her, but tell her story since there was no one to tell it to, and she longed for intimacy as well as catharsis.

The younger unmarried ones congratulated Humeirah along similar lines: "He is so good- looking, just like you. You can't believe how happy I am to hear about this match. He is such a good Memon boy."

Yet others beamed, and said: "You just know when it's the right one, don't you? That's how it is. You just know it, deep down." But Humeirah wasn't sure what that meant. How did one know when it was the right one? There was nothing to compare it against since she had never known any other man before Haider.

The elderly assumed the role expected of them and cautioned her about the evil eye: "You must place a pair of scissors under your pillow when you sleep," said Fatima, Humeirah's aunt. "It will ward off evil. You see, something special is happening to you; not everyone has the chance to get married. People will wish you evil; not just those who are single or divorced, but those who are married. Everyone is jealous of one another these days. Not like those times, long ago, when life was simple and people had good hearts. Why else don't Khalid and Sarah get along? That old woman, you know, Choti Khala, practises sorcery. They say she is the one who cast a spell on them. Trust me, I know what I'm saying."

Another urged her not to take any gift-envelopes because of spells that could cause discord between husband and wife. "Give the envelope to your father or to Haider's parents to open," she advised. "It won't have an effect on them."

Humeirah observed and listened, absorbing and processing, discerning patterns and drawing conclusions, craving for something she still could not entirely fathom, but hoping at the very least that after marrying Haider, she would see much more than that which fitted neatly in boxes.

***

Two days before the wedding ceremony, children crowded around Humeirah as she sat on a carpeted floor of the sitting room in a bright orange shalwar khameez, floral patterns of mehendi drawn on her hands, arms, legs, and feet. Young boys had a crush on her; young girls imagined the day they would be older, seated in that position, enjoying the pomp.

One of the rituals performed on the day was the exchange of gifts and trays between the bride and groom. The bridegroom's relatives initiated it, and each party presented about ten trays to the other.

Haider's relatives however walked into Humeirah's house with sixty-seven trays laden with designer jewellery from some of the most expensive shops of Mumbai; shoes by Jimmy Choo; handbags by Burberry; make-up sets by Bobbie Brown; perfumes by Chanel and Gucci; shalwar khameez sets from the luxurious boutiques of Mumbai and Delhi, and boxes of Patchi chocolates. Since these brands were not available on the local market, everything had been brought by relatives and friends in instalments from several trips overseas. Humeirah's relatives were struck with wonder by how everything was glamorous as well as meticulously planned. As soon as the implications dawned on them, however, they quickly lost their composure: only twenty trays had been prepared for Haider.

Zeba took the lead, and within a few hours and with the help of volunteers, put together trays with chocolates, shaving sets, perfumes and watches, all wrapped in patterned cellophane, and placed beside one another. The guests, including those who had been involved in the last-minute preparations, crowded around the gifts, exhausted but filled with admiration. Zeba was proud of herself, and after Gibran showered her with praise, leaned over and whispered to her husband Aadil that she may as well consider a career as a wedding planner. Aadil nodded, imagining the money it would generate.

That evening, seventy-one trays were sent to Haider's house.

***

Two days later, soon after the maghrib prayer, the nikah was held at the Jummah Masjid in Port Louis. Maulana Faruk read a few verses of the Quran before announcing the mahr, and asked Humeirah's male witness if she consented to the marriage.

The *mahr* was an amount handed over to the bride by the groom. There were many reasons for it; reasons which accommodated the time and space in which they were concocted. The one in circulation, then, was that it provided for three months of maintenance for the woman, should the parties decide to get a divorce. Usually, the bride stated the amount, worked out after assessing her lifestyle and needs—a figure that could be raised at the discretion of the bridegroom.

Among some Memons, it was common that the *mahr* turned into a means of displaying wealth, and among others, their simplicity. In case of the latter, the bride asked for a humble amount calculated to be well below her needs.

Well-to-do Memons scoffed at scant amounts—calling the others low-class cheapskates—while the latter thought of the former as pretentious snobs.

That day, at the Jummah Masjid, Maulana Faruk announced that the *mahr* had been settled at five hundred thousand rupees.

"Such show-offs!" were whispers among those gathered.

***

After the nikah ceremony, guests gathered at the wedding hall of The Oberoi. As planned, Humeirah was the first to arrive, and Haider was to make his entrance an hour later after meeting everyone at the masjid.

The decoration of the wedding hall could have been handled by the hotel personnel, but Shaheen had taken charge of it and sub delegated tasks to volunteers such as Zeba who was asked to handle the flower arrangement. After all, Zeba liked flowers and flower gifts.

That day, silk open red roses with gold-coloured ribbons tied to their stalks were appended on the curtains and the tablecloths in the hall. The red-and-gold was meant to match Humeirah's Bandhani saree, the preferred choice of almost every Memon bride.

When Zeba walked in with her husband Aadil, she took a look at Humeirah who was seated on the stage, and at the backdrop of roses she had ordered, realising to her horror that they were a shade off from the saree. In the hour that followed, Aadil had to reassure her that it was a trivial matter and that nobody would notice, but Zeba remained distraught and inconsolable.

Gibran and Mr. Shah greeted the guests at the entrance where a huge arch of flowers had also been mounted. Mrs. Shah and Shaheen stood right behind, orchestrating the flow and passing the gifts to Ambareen who had been asked to keep watch over them in case they were appropriated by the waiters and waitresses. Many had brought gift envelopes with money since the invitation cards distributed one month earlier had stated the preference. Again, there had been a debate about it, but Haider had had the last say: "We'd rather just have the money. People will bring things we don't like, and we'll end up disposing of them among our drivers and maids."

In the place of customary Bollywood wedding songs, Mrs. Shah had asked for the soundtrack of *The Last of the Mohicans*, after being inspired by the music she had heard at a friend's wedding she had attended in Zürich.

"How pretentious," said one, "these people go abroad and hear European music and come back and try to imitate them. It shows how inferior they feel about their own culture."

Another commented: "How elegant. Better than those Bollywood songs with people running around trees."

"Either way, music is haram," said Fatima. "It's high time these people got to know their religion and stopped attracting the devil to these ceremonies."

Finally, Haider arrived at the hall. But before joining Humeirah on the podium, in conformity with wedding rituals, young and old ladies crowded around him, each expecting an envelope of money before letting him in. Haider knew he had to feign a protest, then hand out one or two envelopes for the crowd to disband.

"How embarrassing," said Shaheen to her mother. "Ki dimoun pou dir! We are at The Oberoi. The tourists who are staying here will think we are from a backward village in India. We should have had a separate hall for the envelope ritual and this unnecessary show."

"Never mind," said Mrs. Shah, peering outside the hall self-consciously, "I should have spoken to Gibran about this. Those *other* Memons indulge in all this nonsense, not us."

Haider came up on stage and leaned over Humeirah. In slow motion, he lifted the veil on her face so that the act could be captured by the cameraman and photographer. Fatima kept nudging Ambareen: "Tell Humeirah to look down. Tell her to look down demurely." Mrs. Shah overheard the comment and stared menacingly at her.

One by one, older guests walked up to the stage, picked up sweets from the coffee table, fed them to the bride and the groom, circled coins and notes around their faces or above their heads, and deposited them onto a cloth placed on the coffee table in front of them. The money would be donated later to charity. The purpose of the ritual, it was said, was to ward off evil.

Haider and Humeirah tried to finish the sweets as quickly as possible to cater for the next guest. Turning to her, he exchanged a smile, and for the first time after the nikah ceremony, addressed her: "Too much sugar, right?"

She smiled.

Fatima observed the ceremony closely and whispered to Zeba: "You know, I won't do this for my son when he gets married. It's *shirk*."

"What's shirk?"

"You don't know? Well, you see, Memons have adopted practices from Hindu traditions; what with the circling of coins and all that agdam bagdam. It's a corruption of Islam. We must get rid of everything that corrupts our religion."

"But this is our *culture*."

"What is more important for you? Your culture, or your religion?"

Zeba was quiet, recalling that the same had been done when she had got married five years ago. Now, as she sat among the guests, looking up at Haider and Humeirah who were seated on the stage, she mulled over what she had just learned from Fatima.

A thought kept haunting her: Was it because of *shirk* that her marriage had been tumultuous from the start?

Fatima continued: "Look at what Nabilah is wearing, showing her stomach and her arms like that. She's so young. She shouldn't be dressing like this."

"I was actually admiring her saree," said Zeba. "She is the modern type. I heard she told her mother she won't marry a Memon. She'll marry whoever she wants."

"Tawbah! What did her mother—what did Zohra—say?"

"Zohra is fine with it."

"Ya'Allah. This Nabilah is too modern. She goes to Lycée, doesn't she? Those French and British private schools in this country are corrupting our youth."

"Yes, they teach subjects like philosophy, psychology, and whatnot, and make people question everything and become rebellious. I've told Aadil there's no way we are sending our Heera there. He doesn't agree with me and says this is the way to go."

Meanwhile, Sarah, who had been privy to the conversation, moved away, and told another friend that Fatima was a hypocrite who didn't practise what she preached, what with all the talk about *shirk*, and yet, the advice she meted to every woman to sleep with a pair of scissors tucked under her pillow on the eve of her wedding night.

***

Waiters swirled around tables, getting ready to serve the four-course western menu. Comments were already circulating among clusters of guests at the wedding. "This was all a bit much," said some. "They could have saved the money and used it to buy a house for the couple," said others. "But they have so much money; they can afford it, so why not?"

Yet others, those who knew, were recounting how, long ago, when the Memons had just arrived in Mauritius from Bhuj in Kutch in the early 1900s, wedding guests would be served rose milk and light snacks, if at all. Later in time, there would be one main course: briyani—the one prepared by Bibi—and maybe carrot or sooji halwa for dessert. Guests—men as well as women— would get together to lend a helping hand in dishing out and serving the food. Some commented on the warmth and conviviality it generated; how it became an occasion to exchange smiles with those who were forgotten; nod at those with whom barely any conversation could be made, or create a spark in someone's heart that would culminate into another excuse for a gathering of a similar nature.

Dinner was served. Haider and Humeirah sat at the head of the only banquet table in the hall. Beside them were the guests of honour—the closest among their relatives. "What a pity that it rained today," said Arif, leaning against the table. Somehow it was more interesting to be near the main table because there were better chances of meeting other guests. "Stop talking and go and eat something, Man!" Haider said.

"No. My stomach's not too good today. I'll eat something later."

"Your stomach? What naughty business have you been up to?"

Haider gave Arif a look and smiled.

A waiter came up to Humeirah. "May I?" he asked, pointing at the empty plate.

"Sure," she replied, as he leaned over to pick it up. "Would you like some dessert, Madame? There's apple pie or banana crumble."

"Banana crumble, please," said Humeirah, realising that she was now a "Madame" after having for long been a "Miss", "Mademoiselle", or "Mamzel".

Arif looked in her direction.

The waiter continued: "Would you like to have it now or later?"

"Now, please." The waiter nodded and moved away.

"Did you hear that, Haider?" Arif asked.

"What?"

"Humeirah wants her banana right now," he chortled. "*Right now*, did you hear? She doesn't want to wait."

Those who were within earshot—including Haider—roared with laughter.

"Let Humeirah have the banana crumble," said a voice, "you can have the apple pie, Haider." It was Aisha, Arif's wife. Everyone looked in her direction. "Some *apple* pie—you know, nice and round." Again, there was laughter.

Humeirah forced a smile.

"What's wrong with you?" Haider whispered. "Relax. Have fun."

Humeirah was taken aback, but also tired. The tension, the excitement and the stress had drained her out. A bride's exhaustion on her wedding day was rarely a topic for conversation, and yet, so much a reality.

***

The first night Haider and Humeirah shared a bed, she barely slept and woke up feeling tired and groggy as she remembered the events of the previous night.

Zeba, who was at the table during the wedding dinner, had noticed that Arif and Aisha's comments had upset Humeirah. She waited for the guests to leave, and while Haider was engrossed in another conversation, placed her hand on Humeirah's arm and said: "I saw what happened. Listen, don't let it upset you. You are married now. Ignore it. It's your first night. Don't spoil it. Remember, only *you* are responsible for your happiness."

Humeirah nodded, crestfallen but relieved. At least someone had noticed and validated her feelings.

Now, the next morning, in the honeymoon suite of The Oberoi, she began to feel uneasy.

*Only you are responsible for your happiness... What did Zeba mean by that? Don't spoil it... Haider was the one who had spoiled it.*

*I shouldn't have given in. I should have spoken to him before we—*

She looked at the man lying next to her. Still a stranger, she thought.

Later, when he opened his eyes, she said: "We need to talk."

Haider remained silent, prompting her to repeat her request.

"Yes, yes. In a while," and after sitting up in bed, stretching his arms, yawning noisily, he reached out for the remote control, fiddled with the buttons, and settled on MTV. Then he flung the remote control to the side and walked towards the bathroom, swinging his arms to the rhythm of the music.

Disconcerted, Humeirah watched him move away. Maybe he hadn't detected the emotion in her voice; maybe he was too content with this new phase in his life to notice how upset she was... Maybe... But the little voice in her head said that Haider couldn't have overlooked something that had obviously affected her.

Haider walked out of the bathroom. He plopped onto the bed and reached out for the remote control.

"I want to talk to you about something that's bothering me," she said.

"Oh yes, what is it?" said Haider distractedly, his eyes fixed on the TV screen.

"I was really upset last night. Those comments that Arif and Aisha made were so offensive."

"What comments?" asked Haider. "Oh, those. Well, you were acting all anti-social..." Turning to fix his gaze on her, he said: "You embarrassed me so much. They were only joking, and you had to act all upset and make them feel so uncomfortable... We were all having so much fun."

"Their remarks were vulgar! How can you turn around and blame me?"

"Vulgar?! Stop exaggerating."

***

For days, during the honeymoon and in the aftermath, the newlyweds argued. By the end of it, the mention of Arif, Aisha, or any incident related to the wedding dinner became a trigger, and it wasn't long before silence set in. Haider didn't wish to admit that he was wrong, nor could Humeirah let go of her consternation.

Many heard about the incident at the wedding dinner, and discussed whether Arif and Aisha were blameworthy, whether Haider should have said something, or whether Humeirah was merely being touchy and oversensitive. When Zareen caught wind of it, she told Humeirah: "I told you, it's never smooth. You must be patient. It took fifteen years for Zakir to change. Haider will change too. In the meantime, her advice was *"Gat li! Gat li!"*. Shower him with love till he is guilt-ridden and compelled to be nice, she said. Humeirah would hear the words resonate in her mind years later.

Fatima launched an investigation to find out if Choti Khala had been invited to Haider and Humeirah's wedding, and if so, whether she had turned up; how long she had stared at Humeirah and with what sort of look, and whether Humeirah had, through a stroke of misfortune, accepted an envelope of money from her.

***

A few weeks later, Humeirah learned that she was pregnant.

Once again, she was under the spotlight. Sour expressions softened; caustic words were replaced with neutral or even reassuring ones. But when *They* said: "Congratulations, we are so happy for you," Humeirah didn't know how to react. Was she meant to be happy when she and Haider were still not talking?

"Things can only get better with a baby in the family, Humeirah," Zeba, said, "Just wait and see, Haider will become more responsible and treat you with more respect."

The belief that children gave marriages stability had been reiterated for as long as Humeirah could remember. But a child, she thought, would only imprison her further.

Yet, *They* were certain of the outcome, as *They* gave advice to those who sought it as well as those who didn't, so that when everyone expressed their boundless happiness, Humeirah merely said: "Let's see what happens."

Perhaps that was the right way of approaching life because there were rules and there were exceptions, and nobody knew when either would apply.

Once more, in noting Humeirah's reaction, *They* concluded that she was quite the oddball.

II

# -The Use and Abuse of Hope-

"There are rules, then there are excep.... is hope." Humeirah

When you are at school, *They* ask the standard question: "What do you want to do when you grow older?"

When you achieve that, *They* ask: "When are you getting married?"

After you are married: "When are you planning to have a baby?"

While you are cradling your firstborn: "When will you have the next one?"

Later, as you're walking in a mall in the company of your children: "Which school will you send them to?"

And one day when your children are enrolled in prestigious universities: "When will your children get married?"

It was almost as if people didn't have much to say and had no choice but to fill the void with these platitudes.

Indeed, Haider decided to get married because *They* had started popping the question. He had a simple desire to be part of something bigger, perhaps of the laws, systems and institutions that made society. It had never crossed his mind that, for some, especially the woman he was about to marry, more was involved.

The only change he underwent after getting married was having to share a bed with someone he barely knew. By then, *They* had already moved on to ask: "When are you planning to have a baby?" But *They* didn't taunt him for long since his wife was pregnant soon after.

***

Every evening, Humeirah would lie in bed, waiting for Haider. She would listen to the noises from the adjoining bathroom: the flushing, flossing, brushing; water flowing out of the tap, followed by creaking noises when he would close it tight. Then there would be the sound of him walking into the bedroom, silence while he would undo his watch, and a thud when he would place it on the bedside table. During that whole time, her heart would be beating loudly.

But Haider would climb into bed, cover himself with the comforter and turn to the side facing the wall, not her. Still, she would wait. Maybe he would finally say or do something, but soon enough, he would fall asleep. His indifference and detachment disturbed her; she believed she had so much to learn, so much to share, so much to talk about. With difficulty, she would try to fall asleep.

During the day, the lack of intimacy and the tense and uncomfortable silence separated them. Humeirah came up with excuses to explain the distance: maybe something was not going well at work; maybe the heavy workload prevented him from being himself; maybe he was trying to adjust to married life. She hoped that in the evening, when Haider was free, he would shed the mask he had put on and devote time to her. She wanted to be privy to the vulnerability, the humanity in him, and she ached to show her vulnerability and humanity to him. Only the display of weakness, she believed, could forge the bonds that united one human being to another.

Time went by and nothing happened. She wanted to give up, but *They* said that she ought to be patient: "Haider will change." But he didn't, so she went back to them and was told that she was not being patient. Then came the day when Humeirah decided to be realistic, realising that she had to do something to reduce the agony.

*Man has invented this thing called Hope to combat negativity; negativity that arises in everyday life through illness, solitude, poverty. That is how the canny businessman turns it to his advantage by providing health products, matrimonial services, and money-lending facilities, promising that which traps people in cobwebs of despair.*

*But Hope turns into man's enemy when he continues to be optimistic against all odds: the terminally ill patient, the fifty-year-old lone woman, and the miserable bankrupt still look up to Hope, otherwise there wouldn't be any point in living.*

*In the end, Hope becomes the noose tied around man's neck, squeezing it but not quite—and this is the state of misery I want to avoid.*

That was why Humeirah made up her mind to stop hoping that Haider would change. Yes, they would sleep in separate rooms.

But emotions are more powerful than reason. Humeirah's decision to sleep alone did not bear the fruits she expected. Alone in bed, she would peer intently at the door of her bedroom, waiting for a knock, a creak. At the least sound of anything, she would strain her ears, expecting Haider to walk towards her and ask: "Why are you sleeping alone?" Then she would imagine looking at him, at the genuineness of the request, and with a smile, climb out of bed, walk with him to their bedroom. Forget conversation; Humeirah craved affection, only that, but it never happened.

Haider did not change, but *They* advised her to wait; Haider did not change after months, but *They* advised her to wait; Haider did not change for years, but *They* told Humeirah that it would happen sooner or later, recounting anecdotes of how the most insensitive people had changed overnight. Humeirah did not know what to do: what *They* said conflicted with what she believed.

Married couples who faced discord and emptiness never underwent change—this, she now knew. The rule dictated that one could not trigger emotions in another if he was by nature so cold.

But it was easier to trust them: *They* were greater in number and spoke with the fervour and conviction of prophets and soothsayers. There was a rule, yes, *her* rule, but *They* had spoken in a way that made her trust in exceptions—these had become her source of hope.

So, every night, Humeirah would stare at the door of her bedroom till she would drift into a deep perturbed sleep.

# III

## -Conflicts-

"To survive, one creates the illusion of being the one who bears the sceptre of truth." The loud voice in Humeirah's head

It was a Sunday afternoon and Haider had planned to host a party so that Shanthi was in the kitchen, preparing for it. Warissah would be sent over for the rest of the day to be looked after by Gibran, her Nana.

As soon as Vijay signalled that he was ready, Warissah grabbed Dolly and the tote bag Shanthi had packed and followed him out of the house.

Humeirah was at her best: Haider had been unusually nice to her, informing her about the number of invitations he had sent, who the guests were, how they were related to him, how relevant or irrelevant they were to his business. She understood that he wanted her to play the perfect hostess, and this time, she was determined to play it well.

But Shanthi was in a bad mood, no longer certain if she was a permanent fixture in the house. Reena, a young maid, had been brought in to assist her. Was Haider trying to replace her? Was the party an opportunity for him to put Reena's skills to the test?

By the first hour, Shanthi complained about her to Vijay: "Doesn't she know she should be more attentive? She is young and naive and doesn't realise she is working for gran dimoun." (Shanthi was not familiar with the term "Memon".) In reply, in a display of intended ambiguity, Vijay just shook his head and remained quiet. But Shanthi wasn't done, and reported to Haider that Reena had already made a few blunders. He was not pleased. The parties were important, and he wanted everything to be perfect. The truth—one Shanthi didn't know, and one which would have helped all parties concerned, had they known it—was that Haider had hired Reena for the image. Two maids were better than one.

That day, Haider, Humeirah, and their guests were seated on the spacious balcony of their house. There was no rule or dictate about where one should sit, yet men and women had instinctively moved away from one another as though they were polar opposites. Shanthi was walking in and out, bringing snacks and sweetmeats for the guests, while Reena was following behind, less confident in her moves than a few hours ago, and yet, determined not to make a mistake.

Once the party was in full swing, women discussed the fate of other women in relationships, men discussed the fate of other men in the working world; women shared tips on beauty, cooking, washing, and cleaning, while men shared tips on frugality, investment opportunities and the cars and properties to buy. The atmosphere was buoyant. Both genders were discussing matters of practical knowledge that were important in the discrete worlds they inhabited.

Occasionally, men and women slipped in a remark and defamed another: "Did you hear about Razia?" Fatima said to Sarah, opening her eyes wide so that the action measured up with the dramatic effect. Instantly, the others turned their attention to her. Fatima loved the attention and the power that came with it. "Who are you talking about?" replied Sarah, "You mean Mahmood's wife, Razia?" Razia was the neighbour Sarah did not like very much, and there was no reason for the resentment. Henceforth, the gossip gave her one.

"Of course, Mahmood's wife," she said, lowering her voice (presumably, the walls had ears). "Something's going on between her and this other guy I know. Would you believe it? What a shame."

A noisy chatter arose and died down. Some of the ladies placed their hands on their open mouths; others shook their heads.

Fatima was not done—the maestro knew that a pause was necessary before her troupe of musicians could engage in a different movement: "And the worst part is that she pretends to be all so saintly and just came back from performing Hajj."

That did it. Razia's reputation had gone to the dogs.

"Who's the guy?" asked Sarah.

Fatima anticipated the question, but if she revealed too much, it would diminish the hold over them so that they would no longer need her.

"Oh, I can't tell you that. I don't want to gossip. It's haram."

"Yes, it makes sense," said Sarah. "I've seen Razia wear nail polish. It means she doesn't pray since you can't do wudu when you wear nail polish."

Humeirah sat in silence, familiar with the gossip that transpired in gatherings; this time however, she wondered about the juxtaposition between a charge of adultery and that of wearing nail polish. But since thoughts were not audible, what showed was the blank expression she wore.

The ladies were not happy. It was clear that Humeirah was not one of them, but an outsider, a spy, almost an enemy, and something had to be done. Fatima looked in Humeirah's direction, now anxious.

Was Humeirah connected to Razia? Maybe a friend? If so, maybe she intended to report it to her—the only reason explaining the silence.

Fatima exchanged a glance with the other ladies. It carried a clear-cut message: "enemy in the camp", so that everyone switched to talking about a recipe one wanted to recommend.

The truth was that Humeirah didn't even know Mahmood's wife, Razia.

Fatima was not done. "What do you think of Samia's marriage to Yasin? Was it a wise move by Anjum and Shahista?"

The ladies around her hesitated since they didn't have an opinion. Fatima chimed in again: "I think it would have been better for her to stay single than marry a Calcattia. What do you think?"

Again, silence.

Fatima continued: "Do you know what Yasin's cousins say about him? That marrying a Memon has gone to his head. *Pli Memon ki li pena!* Then again, I don't think Samia and Yasin are happy. I mean, that's what happens when you marry outside. You don't know what you're getting into. If Samia had married a Memon, if there were problems, someone would have talked to her husband. As I say, once you go outside, there's no control."

"Didn't they have a baby recently?" said Sarah.

"Yes, I think so. Fifty-cents—that's how he will be called when he grows up. Half a Memon. And sometimes it's hard for such people to be accepted in marriage by one-rupee Memons."

A few ladies chuckled, others shifted uncomfortably in their chairs, one whispering to another that Fatima was vulgar and uncouth.

On the other side, Haider and his friends were holding a comparable conversation: "R.... B.... is such a rascal," said Fatima's husband, Hashim. "He will send our country to the dogs. When he appears on TV, he tries to show that he is noble and good. But guess what? He was the one behind that project to construct the M– Motorway. Was it ever completed? No. Guess why? He took all the money for himself. Did you see the Rolls Royce he drives? Where do you think he got the money to buy it?"

Haider continued: "Yeah, long ago it was much better. Those politicians were people who held on to great principles. This country is doomed...just doomed."

Hashim concurred.

"Did you know that R.... B.... entered a second marriage with a woman in Pakistan?" said Arif. "His wife doesn't even know about it. These government ministers are so immoral. Where do you think taxpayers' money goes? They spend everything on women, drugs, and alcohol."

Shanthi and Reena continued to step in and out to remove empty plates and dishes. Then, Haider, Humeirah and the guests got together and sat in a circle, now bereft of the barrier that had separated them earlier. The conversation took a new turn.

"You can't put all Calcattias in the same category," Saabir was saying in reply to something someone had said. "They are *not* all descendants of indentured labourers as many believe. There are people in my family who recount that their ancestors were from Saudi Arabia, and happened to be passing through the port of Surat in India to come to Mauritius, and because of that, were labelled Surti. In the same way, there are Jews who escaped persecution and came to settle here and are now classified under the umbrella term of Calcattia. One more example: a friend, from a supposedly Calcattia family, recently told me that his grandfather was a Moroccan sailor who fell in love with an Indonesian woman, and both eloped to settle down in Mauritius. There is more mixing than you imagine. These divides we have created are misleading and erroneous."

What Saabir had said did not seem to resonate with many. Soon a different question was being tackled.

"Yes, religion is very important," Haider was saying, "since it gives you direction in life."

Hashim said: "There's a story about The Prophet who said that deeds are the most important, so it doesn't matter where you come from, who you are, but it's how you use the power and privilege conferred to you. That's why it's said that the rich will be judged first."

Michael, Haider's childhood friend and then neighbour, interjected: "We have a similar concept of tolerance in Christianity. You all know that sentence: 'Let anyone who has not sinned cast the first stone.' It means nobody is sinless, nobody is perfect. It means we shouldn't judge other people."

"What a great statement!" said Hashim. "Yes, all religions preach good things. Even Jesus was a great man. We Muslims even accept him as one of our prophets. I always say that Christianity is a great religion."

(In the company of conservative Muslims as himself, Hashim would never have said that.)

"Yes," said Michael. "Islam is a great religion too. There's so much in common between the Bible and the Quran. It's quite unbelievable."

(In the company of conservative Christians as himself, Michael would never have said that.)

"What do you believe in, Saabir?" said Haider, turning around to look in his direction. The truth was that Haider didn't really care. He was only playing the good host.

Save for the earlier intervention about Calcattias, Saabir had been quiet during most of the evening.

"I don't know," he said with a shrug. Expressing himself on a subject so contentious, amid a crowd he wasn't familiar with, made him uneasy. "I don't want to take sides," he continued, and eyed the people around.

*Everyone thinks that the religion they practise is the best and the only one that can guide them to reach the Ultimate Goal in life. What is the Ultimate Goal? Nobody knows. Nobody has bothered to give it a serious thought. How can I tell them all this? They won't understand.*

But somehow, after a few hours, the masks of tact, diplomacy and reserve were shed—even by Saabir who had raised a question: "Why did God put a forbidden tree in the Garden of Eden if he didn't want man to be tempted? If you were a parent, would you do that to your child? Would you expose your child to something dangerous and tell him simply to keep away from it just to test his loyalty? It just doesn't sound right. I don't believe in the concept of such a God and the stories that the Judeo-Christian religions, including Islam, have made up about Him."

Michael took Saabir's remark as a personal attack: "God definitely exists," he shouted. As God's advocate, he felt that he had to represent His interests, and felt it important that he play the part. He could just feel how proud God would be of him, like a parent would to a child, and took a deep breath and continued: "Surely, we cannot come from nothing. There's a God out there. It's only logical. Otherwise, we wouldn't be here."

Hashim and Michael had suddenly paired up to fight the same cause—that is, prove God's existence and take a stand against what Saabir had said. Hashim went on: "Michael is right. I can only think that God and only God could have created all those wonders of Mother Nature."

The ladies were quiet. They didn't want to interfere with their men when they were in this mood.

But Humeirah had other plans: perhaps she could clear the haze that clouded the conversation. Still, would *They* understand what she was trying to say?

"Give it a try," urged the little voice.

"Don't you think that we don't have enough evidence to answer the question about God's existence?"

The chatter died down and silence pervaded the atmosphere.

She continued: "Let's focus instead on His function among us: life exposes us to numerous trials and tribulations. When we suffer, we look around and wonder why other people don't. The truth is that some of us suffer, and others less, but the very thought of this arbitrariness feels cruel and unfair so that the best alternative is to believe that we have been *chosen* to suffer and not that there is such randomness and uncertainty in life. And conveniently, we attribute this choice to God. We say that He has a reason for choosing us, and not someone else. Sometimes we even say that He has chosen us because He loves us and wants to test us. It makes life easier to bear. God makes life easier to bear and suffering easier to tolerate."

Those paying attention to her strained themselves to hear her out, more out of curiosity than an interest in what she had to say—what was the bizarre woman everyone deemed mad saying? That evening, many were not sure what Humeirah meant, but the confidence in her tone, the poise with which she spoke, as well as her choice of words—words they had hardly heard—convinced them beyond doubt that she was wrong, because whatever they had heard was different to anything they had heard in their lives. More importantly, their predilection was to dislike and disapprove of her and all that she said and did.

"Are you saying that you don't believe in God?" Hashim asked gravely. He could tolerate the company of atheists, agnostics, and people of other faiths speaking this way; not a Muslim's, and of all people, not his own niece.

"No. I'm saying th—"

"How can you say something like that? Don't you realise how wrong it is?"

"No, Hashim Mamoo. I am just saying that we can't prove the existence of God. There isn't enough evidence out there, and since we can't, well, the next best option is to understand what His function is among us, and whether He fulfils any useful purpose, irrespective of whether He exists."

"Are you still doubting his existence? You are my own flesh and blood. How can you have such thoughts? How dare you."

Humeirah felt frustrated. The atmosphere had grown heavy and unpleasant. A big black screen stood between her and her uncle. Everyone's attention was riveted on them. Haider was also annoyed; the last thing he wanted was for Humeirah to spoil the evening, and jeopardise the budding relationship between his youngest sister and Hashim's son, Kareem.

"My wife is just tired," he interrupted, speaking in a playful tone. Gently, he slapped Hashim on the back and put an arm around his shoulder, and led him away: "Everything's fine," he continued: "She just talks a lot. Everyone knows that. Come on, Hashim Mamoo."

The expression on Humeirah's face darkened.

*People don't necessarily want to have an intelligent conversation. They just want to be heard, and to do that, they interrupt one another, raise their voices, and repeat the same argument more forcefully.*

*In the end, nobody's thoughts are pushed to their limits; nobody is exposed to new ideas; nobody learns anything.*

Humeirah made up her mind that day that she would never again open her mouth to air her thoughts—at least, not in public.

IV

# -In Nana's Company-

"An ugly face needs make-up: that's why man needs religion." The little voice in Humeirah's head.


Warissah was fond of Gibran, her maternal grandfather, who was gentle, spoke to her kindly and treated her with respect. Not many did that. When she appeared at the door with a bag in one hand and a doll in the other, he was there to welcome her, and sometimes, even leaned over and kissed her on the forehead. When she sat on the carpet in the sitting room to play with the toys he had bought, he would join her and turn on the TV, and later, insist on having meals together. For the rest of the time, he sought the help of his maid Kulssum to tend to her.

Warissah was used to being shunted around in the family. Sometimes she would stay with Ambareen, and sometimes with her grandfather, neither of the times crying or complaining about being led away from her parents' house. For her it signified a change of environment, and so long as she was free to carry her doll everywhere, she was content.

"Nana, what will we do today?" she asked, as she stepped into Gibran's house and climbed onto the couch to sit beside him. "In my house, they are cerebrating a party and I have nothing to do."

Gibran averted his eyes from his copy of Le Mauricien and looked at her, wondering how to respond.

"Let's go out," he said.

"Yes, Nana. Where? Where?" She wanted to hug him but held back since he didn't like that.

"Where do you want to go?"

Warissah stared at the ceiling. Sounding disappointed with herself, she replied: "I don-know."

"No. I know," she said, her eyes lighting up. "Balfour Garden."
Gibran looked up and added: "That's the place we should *not* go to now. The roads are busy. There's a concert nearby. I just read about that."

Warissah wondered what the problem was. The car would only move slower than usual. Traffic jams always seemed to be a big issue among grown-ups.

Gibran called for Kulssum. A scruffy lady in her early sixties, with hair curled in shabby tendrils around her face, appeared in a faded green shalwar khameez she washed once a week on Sunday. On that day and the next, she would slip into another one that had also paled and absorbed the colours run into it. In any case, Gibran, her employer, didn't seem to mind it.

To Warissah, for all intents and purposes, Kulssum was not a maid like Shanthi. Every husband had a wife, and Kulssum *had to be* Nana's wife because she did the chores that wives did for their husbands.

"Kulssum," said Gibran, "Warissah wants to go out. Where should I take her?"

"Warissah Baby is just like our Hummy. She loves ice cream."

"Yes, I want ice cream."

"All right," her Nana said. "Let's go to Plaza. We will eat Bhai Mastaan's ice cream."

"What's that? Ee-jay always takes me to Plaza to eat Vona."

"Same thing," said Kulssum.

"Yes, I want to eat Vona," cried Warissah.

Two hours later, after having light snacks, bathing and changing into fresh clothes, Warissah followed Gibran to the Mercedes parked in the garage. Vijay usually opened the car door for her, but with Nana, it was different.

Her small head could barely reach the handle of the car. With difficulty she tugged at the door handle, to no avail. Realising this, Gibran who was already seated, leaned over and opened it from inside. Warissah hopped in and sat down quietly. Another difference was that her Nana showed no objection when she sat in the front seat. Maybe he didn't know the rules. Warissah decided against telling him, since sitting next to him made her feel big.

The drive from the house in Beau Bassin to Plaza lasted twenty minutes because of traffic. The concert near Balfour Garden had affected the movement of vehicles across the area.

At Plaza, Gibran parked in one of the parking bays next to Bhai Mastaan and his white-and-royal blue ice cream tricycle. Then, he climbed out, and accompanied by his granddaughter, placed an order.

Plaza, for many Mauritians, referred to the squarish acre of land in front of the Municipality of Beau Bassin/Rose Hill whose concrete benches were crowded in the evenings with young amorous couples who exchanged more gestures of affection than words. In the afternoon, children gathered and ran on the grass, skipped ropes, flew kites, and played football.

Daily, an elderly round-faced gentleman wearing a blue cap, known to many as Bhai Mastaan, would push his tricycle to the place, station himself in the same spot and sell homemade ice cream in cones and plastic cups. The secret of his coveted recipe, he said, was the milk powder he used. Ambitious housewives tested it in their homes but never came close to matching the flavour. Warissah often said that he sold "the best ice cream in the whole world".

That day, she watched his movements as he scooped out the light green, pink and cream-coloured ice cream from a giant tub of aluminium, stuffed it in a crunchy cone which he topped with a layer of crushed pineapple pieces soaked in rose syrup overnight. Finally, he crowned the concoction with half a teaspoon of coloured desiccated coconut, and leaned over to hand it to Warissah who had been looking up, barely able to follow the steps, but assured that she would somehow get ice cream.

***

"Can I go and play now?" asked Warissah after finishing her ice cream, wanting to run around the square of green.

"No," replied her Nana.

The square was unusually crowded that day, and people wore untucked, tacky shirts and shabby jeans from China and Korea. Everything about them seemed threatening: the bulky metal belts with studs that were coiled around their waists, piercings on their chins, lower lips, temples, eyebrows, and bright tattoos that spiralled dangerously in all directions. The glitter and sparkle of their jewellery stood out against their dark skin.

"They're a bunch of riff-raff," he added. "We should stop coming here."

Warissah didn't know what "riff-raff" meant—it had to signify something bad. "But Eejay lets me run around whenever we come here," she insisted.

"That's wrong. A girl like you shouldn't be mixing with such people."

Warissah thought about her classmate Valérie—a small girl with dreadlocks. Once she had drawn herself and Valérie hand in hand, and had gone on to shade the inside of her outline, leaving her own empty. On seeing it, Valérie had burst into tears, leaving Warissah who had suddenly understood why, feeling guilty.

Warissah also remembered Valérie's father who looked a lot like the men in the square and was always warm and friendly towards her.

It didn't make sense. Gibran's reaction didn't make sense.

"Nana, Dolly doesn't like ice cream very much," she said. Gibran was still observing the "riff-raff" at Plaza.

"Nana, Dolly doesn't like ice cream very much," repeated Warissah.

"Dolly is a doll," replied Gibran, "how can she like ice cream?"

Nana's comment hurt.

It wasn't so much what he had said than the tone he had said it in. Warissah didn't like it when he switched to this mood.

After some time, it grew boring to sit in the car with a silent Nana, and Warissah wanted to run and play; the other children seemed to be having so much fun. "Let's get a DVD, Nana."

"All right."

Gibran drove towards the DVD shop near the bakery in Beau Bassin, and parked in front of it. Both he and his granddaughter got down and went inside. The man at the counter looked at them, awaiting their order.

Warissah said she remembered watching a movie about an extraterrestrial creature; Vijay had told her that it was "science-fiction". She remembered other favourites.

"I want to watch science-fiction movies," she said. The man at the counter cited names of movies in that genre, "*Star Trek*? *Star Wars*?", then looked at Gibran, shook his head and said: "But she's too young for those."

"No," said Warissah, "I want science-fiction movies like *Cinderella* and *Snow White*." The man smiled with Gibran, and after a brief exchange, handed him a copy of *Shrek*.

Back in the car, Gibran glanced at his watch. "I'll pray and then we will go home, OK?"

"All right, Nana."

He drove to the nearby mosque, parked, climbed out, locked the door, and walked towards the sacred place of worship. Warissah sat quietly and stared out at the branches of trees that hung over the car. With the darkening of the day, strange shapes began to form on the dashboard and windscreen, as well as the sides of the door. The shadows were even projected on the cemented wall of a house nearby—they were longer and wider and stretched all the way up.

*Was this what Ustaad Ashraf meant by the shaitan? Did the shaitan appear in this form?*

Wait. Was the shaitan after her?

Since it was time for maghrib prayer, Warissah realised that she ought to have been praying. Her heartbeats grew louder. Effortlessly, she crawled to the rear and stood on top of the seat, her head barely touching the car's ceiling, as she mimicked the movements Ustaad Ashraf had taught her; standing, bowing, prostrating, standing, bowing, prostrating, hoping that the shaitan of the shadows would not come and get her.

V

# -Meat of the Tongue-

"Be a tree, stand alone, be independent, and not a fern, dependent on external structures to flourish." The loud voice in Humeirah's head

Time and again, Humeirah remembered the Kenyan folk tale she had read in her adolescence about a powerful King who was very distraught that his once young, pretty and energetic wife had become thin, pale and listless. He had grown tired of trying the remedies prescribed by the most abled physicians he knew. One day, a cobbler advised him to feed his wife with the meat of the tongue, saying that it would restore her beauty, adding that he had tried it on his own wife.

In despair, the king had all the animals in the kingdom butchered, and fed his wife their tongues at every meal. The Queen only grew uglier. In a fit of rage, he ordered the cobbler to exchange wives with him, which the cobbler did, but sadly and reluctantly. A few months later, the King was even more enraged to find out that his new partner had grown ugly, and his wife, now with the cobbler, was as beautiful as ever. He ordered his wife back to the palace and asked her to explain the change. She said that the cobbler had fed her the meat of the tongue every day. The King glared at her—he had done no less the same!

Eventually, the Queen explained the significance of the meat of the tongue. Every day after work, the cobbler would sit at the dining table with her and tell her about how he had spent the day, sharing his joys, sorrows, hopes and apprehensions, thereby feeding her the meat of the tongue.

The story had left a lasting impression on Humeirah. Like many of her age, she had started dreaming about the relationship she aspired to share with a man. Later, after marrying Haider, when she realised she was not happy and fulfilled, she remembered the folk tale, wishing more than anything that he could spend time with her after work, baring his heart, sharing his joys, sorrows, hopes and apprehensions.

On one such day, a few months after their marriage, she decided to join him for a cup of tea while he was watching TV.

"Did you have a nice day?" she asked, stressing the sincerity in her tone in order to convey candour. Haider uttered an acknowledging: "Mm."

"Quick!" advised the little voice.

"So, what is the project you are working on?" she asked. "I overheard you talking about it yesterday on the phone."

Haider's eyes were riveted on the TV screen, and he kept fiddling with the buttons of the remote control. "Nothing. Just another project."

"Tell me about it."

Silence.

"Where did you have lunch today?"

"Why are you asking pointless questions?" he shouted. "I ate wherever I chose to eat."

Humeirah turned and stared at the TV screen.

*Why would such a man want to get married?*

*This is meaningless; nothing binds us to each other. If either one of us is not around, it makes no difference to the other.*

Instead of moving away, she clung to the belief that she could make her way into his heart.

"What have I done? Let's talk. There's so much we can do to make this work."

"What do you want? You are never happy. Leave me alone. You always complicate everything."

Humeirah remembered what he was alluding to. They were watching the news one evening, and in one of the specials, a woman related sordid experiences of being the victim of a finance scam. The only reason she was retelling her story, she added, was to warn people because she cared. Humeirah had turned to Haider, and said: "People say they care, but while it is possible to care for a specific individual, is it possible to care for people at large? Caring for collectivities sounds so far-fetched. Don't you think that in claiming that she cares, she is in truth disguising the cruder desire of sharing her story of victimhood?"

Haider had looked up from his cup of tea. "Stop complicating everything, Humeirah. You read into absolutely *everything*. Sometimes things are just as they are. The woman says she cares, so she cares. What more is there to analyse?"

But out of naivety—or despair—she didn't stop, like now, drawing nearer to him and placing her hand on his. "We don't have to argue. Let's work on this."

There was a blow. A hard one so that she fell to the ground. Once, she knocked a flower vase and the remote control that was on the couch dropped onto the floor and the battery cover slipped out—an image etched in her memory, the sight of which, even on benign occasions, would trigger a reminder of these moments.

"Shut up. Shut your bloody mouth up."

She wouldn't—she *couldn't*. She could barely hear him amid her tears and sobs.

"Please listen to me," she would sputter, "Hear me out first."

He *had* to, especially when she was appealing to him so earnestly, but the blow... the blow... It had come as a shock.

*Why?*

He would go back towards her, force her stretched out arms to the ground, sit on her body, pinning her legs between his. Effortlessly, he would wrest control of her body. Then, with one hand, he would hold both her arms to make sure that she posed no physical threat to him, and with the other, cover her mouth with a rough clasp. One could only hear her muffled cries and see her body, powerlessly writhing in pain.

"Shut up, I said. If you don't shut your bloody fucking mouth, I won't let you go."

She wouldn't.

"Please? Please..." she would say, whenever he moved his hand away from her mouth to find out if she had calmed down.

The sobbing was the one thing he couldn't stand, so that it would prompt him to raise his voice higher and utter the threat in harsher terms. At times he would place his hand not on her mouth, but her throat, squeezing it and watching her struggle. Every time this would happen, Humeirah would reprimand herself for not learning the rules of the game.

The rule was that he would never change; arguing with him was pointless. The wisest would be to shut up, but she wouldn't because this was all about human beings, and because of that, there were exceptions, and therefore, hope.

Haider would get up from the floor, from on top of her body, from the pillow-like softness, and stride out of the room with gigantic confident steps. Humeirah would be crying, trying with all her might to suppress the pain; trying with all her might to shut down her mind and thought process, to no avail.

*If only there was an outlet to vent my distress.*

*But what's the point? Who wants to listen to this sob story? People express their pain so that they are given some reassurance, and so that when they hurt again, there is someone by their side.*

*And yet, there is nobody. Nobody will turn up, nobody will understand. This is an icy-cold world.*

Meanwhile, Shanthi would have heard every bit of it—but it was not her business. When it happened in the evenings, she knew she had to expect it to be louder; especially when it was time for bed. The blows as well as the shouting and crying would prevent her from falling asleep, so that she would have to press a pillow against her ears, or turn on the radio. But Humeirah never failed to be louder.

# VI

## -Pretences and Instincts-

"How often do we disguise our vile and selfish emotions with dignified-sounding reasons?" Humeirah

The next day, early in the afternoon, Vijay stopped the car at the supermarket in Trianon, and after Humeirah climbed out, he drove away to park and wait for her.

*Claustrophobia.*

The word resonated in her mind.

She entered the supermarket, and it was crowded—how strange on a Tuesday.

Claustrophobia was the torture she underwent when, weighed down by emotion, she endured the conflict between who she was and what she was trying to be. Then, the room she would seek refuge in would feel stuffy; as would the house and the garden, as well as conversing with Shanthi or Vijay. Her solace? Loitering in wide expanses of physical space—like this mall.

The people around her, especially their proximity, reassured her. They, seemingly engrossed in their worlds, had no time to hurt, to sigh, to pause, and whose apparent indifference to the questions that haunted her, felt like balm.

Why did she worry?

Why did she worry when *They* didn't?

*Why am I caught up with my emotions? These people suffer too. They too go through perpetual cycles of happiness and sadness. And yet it's so easy for me to think that I am the only one suffering; so easy to close myself up in a bubble and believe that nobody understands what I go through; so easy for every sufferer to feel that his or her pain is the worst.*

In the supermarket, Humeirah broadened her focus from the thing and the individual—the one—to the whole, taking in as much as she could at one time. She didn't see the man or the woman, but crowds of them. She didn't see the item on the shelf, but the entire gamut of products on display.

*How often do we lose track of the whole while focusing on the specific? And more importantly, what do we miss in doing that?*

As she walked through the aisles, husbands stood beside wives, or lagged behind, some with more sterile expressions than their counterparts. Mothers and fathers walked next to their children, some in silence, some tending out explanations, some preoccupied with controlling their tantrums. Young couples who didn't know where to go and had instead chosen this space to wander, wore bashful smiles and behaved discreetly, both in action and emotion. The more purposeful shoppers scanned the shelves, making sure their selections suited their needs, sometimes coming back to the same spot, obsessively, compulsively, comparing price tags, switching and replacing items.

Humeirah thought about how institutions such as these were set up out of nowhere, how people flocked to them so naturally, and how function matched need in perfect symmetry. Then, treading in no direction, observing the contents of baskets and trolleys filled mostly with consumables, she thought about another cycle familiar to man: the one involving ingestion, digestion, and egestion.

*Cycles. Cycles everywhere.*

*What was the point?*

In line with the thought, what she now saw before her was a crowd of automatons, functioning to fulfil needs they had no control on.

How disappointing. How much agency did we really have over our lives, despite the claims we made to a better understanding of ourselves, having meticulously documented three thousand years of history?

Humeirah walked out empty-handed.

The patterns of behaviour she had just witnessed in the supermarket, she told herself, were permanent and unchanging, so that in the end, despite the time and space we occupied, and despite the feeling of uniqueness we longed to believe in, there was something terribly common and *ordinary* about us, because what was happening here, had happened and was happening in every country; what was happening here had happened and would go on to happen in every era.

Surely the torture she was going through by questioning everything was also futile, as was the pain she was enduring trying to fit in.

Didn't she, like everyone, fit an archetype? Weren't there therefore other people like her?

Yes, surely. Only that she couldn't discern who they were, since thoughts were not inscribed on one's face or body, and there was no outward measure to single out who was who.

Then again, would it benefit her if she knew, and if so, how?

And as much as there were cycles of what was happening around her, of what she stood for, weren't emotions, too, as whimsical? Didn't it then appear silly to be happy when happiness could be snatched away? Or cry over pain because pain too was ephemeral?

So why did people bother?

Why did she?

Humeirah was conscious that she was seeking a means to overcome what she had endured the previous day. Her pain *had to* appear insignificant; she *had to* find a way to move on.

While walking towards the parking lot, she realised she had been happier standing at the far end of the prison cell; at least it had given her the impression that the iron bars were a distance away, and that a new world lay beyond. It gave her hope. But now that she had come closer to the bars, she could already scan what was beyond. The answer was: there was nothing.

*Nothing.*

Henceforth, even if she succeeded in escaping this prison, there was nothing that could make life better. Those who spoke about reforming prisons, were merely decorating them, and those who spoke of revolutions were only creating new ones. Were we just doomed to live in them, one way or another?

So, how long could she go on hoping?

At different intervals in her marriage, she recalled how she had believed that the best way to deal with her problems was to pretend to be someone different. That was why, in the beginning, she had played the role of the wife that Haider desired; the wife who truckled to him, and showered him with respect and admiration. That's what he wished for, didn't he?

Zeba's husband Aadil had wished for that too, and Zeba had changed to be that, and more. Maybe that was why she was content.

In the first few months of their marriage, Haider would say: "I have thought about life very seriously, Humeirah. People say that I am very mature and sensible. I have struggled to get here. I am respected, you know. Yes. I already own two executive cars and have investments in six prime property areas, and I am only thirty. I know I have a long way to go to get *there*, but I have already achieved a lot, no doubt."

Humeirah would look at him intently and smile. It was the authoritative look in his eyes, the confidence in his gestures. She believed that her smile would be sufficient to convince him, and establish the intimacy and cohesion she longed for. But what she had failed to realise was that human beings had evolved from beasts only recently: their instincts were still sharp and powerful, so that Haider could sense the deception. He stopped falling for it and began to detect other instances when she would feign emotions and gestures of praise and admiration. Slowly, he took a distance and stopped confiding in her, and that was the end of it.

Yes, honesty was easier.

Humeirah had thought about Jaques, the character conjured up by Shakespeare, who had said: "All the world's a stage and men and women merely players." For the first time, she understood what it meant.

What she yearned was to be around someone who would let her be the spectator in a dark theatre, oblivious to any etiquette of conduct, laughing and weeping when she felt like it. Being married to Haider and watching her skills give way to exhaustion, had taught her that she was a bad player, and would forever be one.

Humeirah walked to the parking lot and spotted Vijay.

"What did you buy, Madame?"

Humeirah could see how intently and seriously he meant it and avoided his eyes.

"Nothing."

"I thought you said you wanted to buy Chinese balm."

"Yes. A balm, Vijay," she said, wishing she wasn't wound up in these situations, bared to the world and its people, struggling between honesty, reserve and tactfulness. "I think I found it..."

The driver shook his head. *Poor woman.*

# VII

## -The Purpose of Communication-

"You're only lonely the day you realise nobody shares your opinions." Humeirah

"Can you read this to me, Ti?" asked Warissah, holding out a book. They were in the kitchen.

"I am busy right now, mo gater. In any case, I don't know how to read," replied Shanthi.

Warissah looked disappointed.

*All adults knew how to read. Why not Ti?*

Shanthi noticed her expression.

"Your mother reads so many books. Why don't you ask her?"

Warissah looked up at her.

"Yes, go upstairs and ask her, but first, finish your breakfast. I am heading upstairs now. I have cleaning to do." Warissah nodded.

***

Humeirah was in bed, reading, waiting for the rain to subside so that she could go for a walk. She had heard Shanthi's footsteps on the staircase, followed by her movements in and out of the adjoining rooms, dusting and mopping. Now the clanking of her metal bangles evoked images in her mind: the maid raising or lowering her arm, dropping, or lifting something, pushing and pulling the pail of water. Humeirah could barely concentrate.

There was a knock on the door. It couldn't be Shanthi—she could still hear the noise of her bangles.

A timid Warissah appeared at the door, Dolly pressed tightly against her chest. A rare sight.

The little one approached the bed and handed a thin book to her mother. "Can you read to me, please?"

Humeirah nodded, overwhelmed.

Warissah climbed into bed and waited for her mother to read the abridged version of Heidi.

As the story unfolded, Warissah snuggled closer to her mother until her face rested on her arm. The feeling was new, and Humeirah wanted to draw her daughter close to her. But what if she turned away?

With a big lump in her throat, Humeirah barely managed to get through the book, stumbling on words, missing a page or two.

"Mummy, Ti's *bang-ges* make too much noise, right?"

Taken aback, Humeirah chuckled.

"Yes, but let's ignore that, shall we? Heidi's story is more interesting."

Warissah nodded, clearly reluctant to revert her attention to the book.

"What is inside?" she asked.

"What do you mean, Warissah?"

"What is inside Dolly?" Warissah shook her doll and the metal bead tinkled.

It was Humeirah's turn to shake the doll. "I don't know, Warissah, but I think it's a small bead."

"Will it come out?"

"If you break the doll, yes, but surely you don't want to do that..."

"No, Mummy, never. Let's read."

Humeirah nodded and reverted to reading out the story of young Heidi and her interactions with her grandfather, Clara and Peter, hung up on the moment; hung up on "Mummy".

After a while, Warissah asked: "Why doesn't Peter like Clara?"

"Because Heidi loves Clara. Peter is jealous of her."

"Why?" said Warissah, with eyes wandering around the room.

"Because Heidi loves her. Peter is jealous."

"Why?"

Maybe Warissah doesn't understand the concept of jealousy, thought Humeirah, and resumed reading. When it ended, the little one took the book, hopped from the bed, said a polite Thank you, and walked out.

Humeirah watched her four-year-old leave. For the first time, she did not try to justify the regret. Instead, she spent the rest of the day reading the book she had started that day, all the while recalling what had happened earlier, struggling not to feel overwhelmed.

***

Just before sunset, there was a knock on the bedroom door. Humeirah wondered if it was Warissah.

Shanthi waited for an answer and then walked in. She wanted to know if Humeirah wanted dinner.

"No, but I am going out for a bit."

"It's raining."

Humeirah continued to slip on a pair of flat shoes and a cotton sweater. The maid looked at her.

*I've had enough of this woman. She's just an idle person with an idle mind who indulges in idle activities.*

Outside, wild bushes and trees grew haphazardly over the vast expanse of land. Since everyone trusted their neighbours, each house was separated by low walls or manicured bamboo—the higher walls barricading the exterior were for outsiders. And although the empty space around each structure meant more privacy, it also signified more isolation.

Humeirah stepped outside and walked straight ahead, towards the wilderness. Soon, she was drenched and cold, but it didn't matter. The intimate feeling of a foreign particle against her skin felt gratifying as she listened to the muffled sound of rain falling on overgrown grass. Tonight, she was part of this, of nature, and belonged.

As she passed a row of shrubs, she bent over to touch their moist leaves, and with her thumb and forefinger, massaged and applied pressure on them, feeling their varying texture. It felt similar to touching the auricle of her ear on a cold morning after a shower.

Feeling, without the need to reason. If she had to describe what she felt every time, words could deny her of the experience—or *reinforce* it, she realised as an afterthought.

Humeirah straightened up and looked in the distance. The outlines of the dark trees were clear, and light from the moon as well as from a nearby lamp projected shadows on various spots on the ground. Through the trees, against the backdrop of the fine leaves and their patterns, she watched raindrops sheared by the force of the wind.

Humeirah realised how lonely she was. The warmth she had experienced from Warissah that day had left a vacuum; one she now yearned to fill. Her thoughts reverted to what she was witnessing. How she wished she could enjoy the beauty before her with another. Haider came to her mind, but she was reminded of the sour look he gave her every time, like a dagger stabbing her heart; like the leaves she was looking at, probably felt, when the rain grazed them with razor-blade sharpness.

The only way she could fit in, she thought, was if she reached a point of agreement with others. But what were the chances? When she had to share her thoughts, she was like a little girl hiding behind a screen, anxiously stepping forward on tiptoe, ready to dart back to her hiding place in the face of opposition. More often than not, Humeirah found herself darting back.

"Humeirah?"

The voice took her by surprise. Zeba's towering figure strode towards her. The rain had reduced to a mere drizzle, but still, Zeba was carrying an umbrella.

Humeirah and Zeba had gone to the same school and had had their firstborns in the same month, but they were not particularly intimate. These were mere coincidences but Zeba pointed them out at every opportunity, as if filling the void of conversation between them. Humeirah found them tedious at first, then reconciled herself to the thought that it added levity to their exchanges.

"I saw you from my bedroom window," said Zeba. "I was worried that someone was walking in the rain, and that too, at so late an hour. That's when I realised it had to be you and decided to bring an umbrella, just in case."

Humeirah smiled at her.

"How are you Humeirah? How's Haider? How's Warissah? I haven't seen you in ages. We're cousins as well as neighbours; we went to the same school and had our firstborns in the same month and the same year, and yet we hardly meet."

"Everything's still the same, Zeba. Warissah and Haider are both fine. I was home all day and was claustrophobic, so I thought of coming out. It's beautiful out here in the dark, with the rain pouring."

"Yes, it's nice," said Zeba, distractedly.

"Quick!" said the little voice in Humeirah's head.

"How are you, Zeba? How are Aadil and Heera?"

"They're fine, Humeirah. Heera stood first in her class this year, so we have decided to take her to Disneyland. How is Warissah? I heard Warissah also did very well in her exams. Heera adores Warissah, you know. They even share their lunch at school. But I don't want Heera to go back to that school after this year. Did you hear about the scandal involving another student in their class? His name is Suhaib."

"No, Zeba, I don't. Who is Suhaib?"

"Long story. I'll tell you some other time. I try to avoid negative talk in the evening because it affects my sleep, and then my mood the whole of the next day. But yes, apparently, the boy was being abused and mistreated at home and in school, and no one denounced it till an inspector noticed that he was unduly glum. Now there's a police inquiry into the matter, and the teachers as well as Suhaib's parents are under scrutiny. Many others have decided to remove their children from there. Anyway, let's not discuss it. Like I said, I avoid negative talk in the evening. I wanted to tell you that Heera enjoys Shanthi's cooking so much. Just imagine, she even told me that I need to learn a few recipes from her."

Humeirah smiled.

"Yes, Shanthi is a good cook."

The silence was awkward. What more could she say about her daughter? And about the maid? What else could she talk about?

"Humeirah, I know you're not very happy. People say so many things about you. They say that you suffer from mental problems, but know that I don't believe them. I have known you for a long time. How insane of them to say such things. I am here if you want to talk."

Humeirah peered at her interlocutor, hesitating. Here was a woman she had known for a long time who might understand, who might be forgiving, so maybe it would not be a bad idea.

Humeirah tiptoed from behind the screen.

"To be honest, Zeba, maybe they are right. Maybe, on and off, I am a bit depressed because I feel I just don't have answers to my many questions. And then, I see so many things, but I can't do anything about them. Haider and I don't communicate much. I feel very...lonely."

Silence.

"Well, Humeirah, you must reach out to Haider and speak to him. Women must make sacrifices and sometimes that involves patience, and believe it or not, pain and suffering. Men are always difficult, and like my mother says, they're all like children. Listen, if you are patient, Haider's heart will soften, and he will start understanding you. He is your husband, how can he not love you?"

Humeirah darted back and disappeared behind the screen. She waited for a while, bearing the awkwardness, and then said: "I need to get back now. It's late."

"No problem. Like I said, you can come over any time to talk."

Humeirah and Zeba exchanged a long and sincere hug, Zeba believing she could solve Humeirah's problems; Humeirah, knowing that even if Zeba didn't understand her, at least meant well.

Humeirah made her way back to the house. Again, it had started raining heavily; water gracefully received by the wilderness. Raindrops travelled along tree trunks and branches, bounced off flowers and leaves, and poured into the ground, forming new streams and rivulets that varied in force and flow and merged with something more potent in another cycle known to man.

From the outside and from above, everything seemed well-organised and harmonious, as every element of nature was engaged in a coherent and symbiotic dialogue.

# VIII

## -The Law of Minimum Effort-

"Hanlon's razor: The idiot by sheer luck often ends up playing the right card." Humeirah

The night was at its peak so that the bedrooms of many homes sheltered the limp, vulnerable and still bodies of men, women and children in awry positions. Humeirah's body was curled up in a foetal position, so that one would have thought her peacefully asleep.

Her body entered a rapid convulsion; her eyes opened abruptly. Her brow and scalp were clammy, and her nightdress stuck to her skin. Beads of sweat trickled out of her pores, especially her forehead and the rest of her upper body.

It was the same dream.

Sensing danger, she would be calling out for help—the one instance in her life when she desperately needed someone to come to her rescue. But, in the dream, there would be no sound, so she would take a deep breath, pluck up courage once more and give it another try. Still nothing. Again and again, she would exert herself to no avail. It was the fear, the panic, the despair of wanting to communicate with the world. Sometimes she would feel threatened by the possibility of dying, but on waking, tell herself that it was the least of her worries. The end was never an issue; it was the pain preceding it that she feared. She had read that man was not scared of what he knew, had control over, or could predict, but that which he didn't. That's why he sought to find explanations for everything, and on finding them, embraced them whole-heartedly, even when they were obviously flawed.

This thought had consoled her at first, till she underwent a change and formed her own opinion on the matter: she realised that death was itself unpredictable, so that the anxiety surrounding it was intertwined with the fear of existence.

When she was wide awake, Zeba's words from their last encounter rang in her ears: *He is your husband, how can he not love you?*

*People think along such simplistic lines. A husband is supposed to love his wife. What if he didn't?*

*When I was pregnant, nobody asked how I felt; instead, they jumped to the conclusion that a woman had to be happy. If I showed any other emotion, They would have told me to shut up and not think too much.*

*They also thought that living with one's in-laws was the worst a newly married woman could experience, and yet, in the first few days of my marriage, I enjoyed living with Haider's parents and Ambareen. Their presence was so warming, and I thrived being in a family setting, especially since it introduced the levity we badly needed after the rough start. Still, everyone kept feeling sorry for me, and counted the days till Haider finally announced that the renovations to the new house were complete and we could move in.*

Perturbed, she turned over to face the other side of the wall, but soon, regained a feeling of peace.

*Maybe people don't want to put much effort in thinking.*

*Maybe it takes too much out of oneself to push reasoning to another level, questioning generalisations and sweeping statements, admitting exceptions to rules, and looking beyond the simplistic black-and-white of everything.*

*Maybe it's easier to put in the minimum of effort in thinking. A husband must necessarily love his wife, a pregnant woman must necessarily be happy, a woman living with her in-laws must necessarily be tortured. But numbers determine the norm. The way they behave is more prevalent than the way I do.*

*I know that the lines that separate black from white are merely imaginary; that they have been constructed in language and by that token, in thought, and that these boundaries give us the false sense of comfort and security.*

*That's why, while everything beyond these rules—dogmas—seems impossible to them, everything beyond them seems possible to me—and that's why I seem incapable of taking a firm stand on anything.*

That night, Humeirah could not go back to sleep. Indeed, she had successfully resorted to reason to understand what was going on around her, why people were the way they were, and how different she was from them. But this, she knew, had *not* rid her of the recurrent nightmare.

Indeed, in the daytime, reason had the power to pacify as well as the ability to bring words together to make up something logical and appealing, but at night, it surrendered itself to a compelling power whose origin remained unclear. The result was the absence of reason, the il-logical-ity, the *non*-sense of her nightmares.

Reason, thought Humeirah, was a mere construct devised by man to fool himself into believing there were answers and solutions for everything, and therefore, *just another coping mechanism.*

But, however limited a tool, reason, she knew, was one of the few means she had to establish a connection with the world.

# PART IV

# Mourning

# I

## -Piecing up the Puzzle-

"Once bitten, tw...barely shy." Humeirah

"Humeirah," said Haider, as he walked into the bedroom at a pace that denoted urgency. If one paid attention to the way he had called out her name, one would have caught a hint of kindness in his tone.

Humeirah was in a chair by the bed, immersed in a book that few would pick for leisurely reading. Clad in a plain white shalwar khameez and a multicoloured dupatta, she was waiting for Vijay to pick her up and drop her at Shaheen's place. Her husband's tone had caught her by surprise, but she was more intrigued by his unexpected appearance. He never did that—at least not at this time of the day.

The thought crossed her mind that maybe, just maybe, this was it—the day her husband had decided to alter the course of their relationship.

"Humeirah," he repeated, leaning over her to touch her shoulder. That too was unprecedented.

"Yes?" she replied, looking up at him.

"Humeirah, your father...Your father." He shook his head.

It took a few seconds to register. "Papa?"

Haider nodded and continued to look at her. It was his eyes.

"Oh," she added, her voice dropping. She looked down at the open book and stared at it blankly. Just before Haider had walked in, she had been deep in thought, lost in the ideas contained in the book. Now it seemed as if she had been grabbed from that world, shaken up violently, and hurled into a strange one that everyone said was the real thing.

She searched for emotions in her heart. She tried to think about what her father's death implied for her, for Warissah, for the family—still nothing.

Finally, she asked: "How did it happen?"

"In his sleep." Haider leaned back. "It happened quickly. He didn't suffer."

Humeirah put her book away, stood up, and headed towards the door, then hesitated.

"Should I change into something else?"

"No, what you're wearing is plain enough. Let's go."

Haider followed her out of the room, down the staircase and to the car in the driveway.

***

The night before, while watching TV, Gibran had had his dinner, read the newspaper, and then retired to bed, exactly how he did daily. Somehow that evening—which had started as any other and promised to end the same way—an event, possibly of infinitesimal importance in the greater sphere of things, had disrupted the flow of events which in the long run, would exert an impact on the lives of many.

All day, he had had a tingling feeling in his arms and legs and mild pain in his chest. The next day, before sunrise, at the time he usually woke up to pray, he still lay in bed, inert and motionless.

A few hours later, it was Kulssum who wondered why she had not heard Gibran's diurnal trudge into the kitchen to ask for a cup of tea. She waited a while after knocking on the door of his bedroom and when there was no reaction, barged in, expecting the worst.

Gibran was in bed in a pair of pale blue pyjamas she had ironed the day before. It was clear what had happened. A panicked Kulssum phoned Haider, not knowing what else to do, and in turn, he had called on the family doctor, who after examining Gibran, announced that he had suffered a massive heart attack.

Vijay was now driving Humeirah and Haider to Gibran's house. Humeirah discerned a trait in Haider she had never seen before. Calling everyone one by one to announce his father-in-law's demise, his tone and expression spelled kindness, almost as if he had received tidings of his own father's death. How she wished he was always like that. Now that her father had passed away, would he be different towards her? Would he be affectionate since she had lost the only parent she had?

Humeirah began to harbour hope, but the little voice in her head warned her against it.

By the time Haider and Humeirah arrived at Gibran's place, relatives and friends dressed in white and other pale or sombre colours, were already present; others continued to pour in. Men wore kurtas while ladies were in shalwar khameez. Jewellery and makeup had been laid aside, and everyone had changed into the simplest clothes. Bodily movements and gestures had become unusually slow, and everyone wore a glum expression. Even the younger ones were not their bubbly selves—some mimicked their elders without much effort; others became more mindful only after being berated, realising that play and merriment were inappropriate and antithetical to the mood and setting.

Those who cared to wonder were aware that this display of lethargy—nearly a brooding over life—was a response to the abrupt apparition of Death. Mundane activities that would have kept them going had been put on hold so that they could slow down and pause and ponder on what was imminent for them too.

"What a great man he was," exclaimed Hashim as he stepped into the house and headed towards Haider, taking his hand in his.

"Yes, such a good man," said Michael who followed behind. "Always gentle, always had a good word for everybody." Michael had decided to attend the funeral because he was Haider's friend. He had first met Gibran at Haider and Humeirah's wedding, and then bumped into him once after that at the supermarket.

"He had a tough life," said Haider. "His wife passed away when he was quite young, and he never remarried."

"Yes," said Hashim, "My dear sister—his wife—adored him. They had the most loving relationship. It's unfortunate that she died abruptly so that he had to raise their daughter on his own, which we must admit he did devotedly. He was also very attached to his granddaughter. Such a good father and grandfather. A great man."

There was silence.

Hashim shook his head and added: "It's tragic. Heaven awaits him. There's no doubt about it."

The cluster of men around Haider dispersed and other people walked in, exchanging a word or two, or simply touching his shoulder. In the sitting room, a new cluster was formed, giving out orders, preparing to perform rituals for the burial.

Humeirah didn't go unnoticed. She was what was left of the deceased. Perhaps *They* wanted to live the moment through her, but more likely, *They* were waiting to witness the reaction expected of a daughter who had lost a father.

"Look at her," whispered Fatima to Sarah, as both had their eyes riveted on Humeirah, "she is not even sad. I didn't even see *one* tear roll down her cheek. What sort of daughter is that? To think that Gibran did so much for her and didn't remarry just to take care of her. He spent so much on her, devoted his time to her, brought her up with so much love, and even took care of her daughter on the weekends. What an ungrateful woman!"

"Yes," agreed Sarah. "You know what I heard?"

Fatima narrowed her eyes. "What?"

"She doesn't do anything at home. She is always depressed. Her daughter Warissah is not a normal child, and most likely mentally disturbed as a result of neglect. Humeirah doesn't know how to take care of her. Apparently, she lies in bed all day, eats there and doesn't shower. She doesn't even clean the house and the maid is forced to do everything. Her husband is disgusted with her. She doesn't cook for him, so he goes out and eats in restaurants. I heard that they don't even sleep in the same bed...if you know what I mean. That's why they have only one child."

"Who told you that?" asked Fatima.

"I can't tell you."

"Tell me. Why are you hiding it from me?"

"OK, but you won't tell anyone, right?"

"Yes, come on. This stays between us."

(Of course, it wouldn't.)

"Vijay, their driver told Kumar, my driver."

"Ah!" It was important for Fatima to know where the information originated so that she could assess its reliability. Now, she had another story to keep track of.

She turned to Sarah: "You know, I always tell my friends about how we met the first time in Majeed and Sahana's wedding and couldn't stop talking! It's as if we had always known each other. We should meet again. Why don't you come home for a cup of tea? I'll be making some hot bhajias with tamarind chutney next Wednesday."

Fortunately, Humeirah was not within earshot. From a corner, she was watching men and women walk past her. A few touched her shoulder, cheek, or arm, and whispered reassuring words; others embraced her, sometimes warmly, sometimes perfunctorily. Humeirah noticed Haider's parents, Ambareen, Shaheen, Fatima, Zareen, Sarah, Zeba, Hashim and Michael, and people she had not seen in a long time. Warissah was huddled up against Shanthi, holding Dolly, looking around, oblivious to what had happened to her Nana. Humeirah noticed her and had a flashback of herself at that age.

Her thoughts went back to Haider and his conduct earlier: yes, she did entertain the hope that things would change for the better. She had the desire to change, to be a good wife and do what was needed to make her marriage work, even if she didn't agree with everything. Thoughts of how Haider would truly love her, how they would go on outings as a family, and how both would know what was happening in each other's mind and heart, gave her hope.

During this time, she was not stirred by the movement of people or by what had prompted it, so that her face remained expressionless. She did wonder at her own indifference but thought that she had maybe grown used to the idea that sooner or later, her father would die. In the past, when he had meant everything to her, she had often imagined how it would feel the day she would see his lifeless frame and it had made her melancholy, but as time had gone by and detachment set in, the feeling and reaction had both abated.

Now, as Gibran's body lay in bed, Humeirah sat next to him, her head bowed. According to the rituals, Gibran's body would soon be shifted onto a bedsheet and carried to a long wash basin designed to clean dead bodies. She noticed how the wrinkles on his face and neck had eased out and how his face looked more youthful. It was easy to conjure up various theories about his appearance and what it signified: somebody who walked in commented that there was *noor* on his face—a glow deemed holy—and pointed it out to another who thought he too could see it. The Naked Emperor would have been happy to keep the company of such people, thought Humeirah.

The room was getting warmer. Nobody had bothered to turn on the air conditioner for the man in the room. If he was alive, he would have thrown a tantrum. Humeirah noticed a pair of dark trousers on a rack fixed to the wall which he had probably worn the day before, the last day of his life, and had hung there—to think that he had done it for the last time.

What would be the fate of his personal belongings and the things he had grown attached to, like the platinum watch on the bedside table? For a long time, he had coveted one after learning about a hadith prohibiting men from wearing gold, giving up all aspirations of owning a gold watch like most of his peers did.

What was Humeirah to do with it now? What would have been his wish? But did it really matter?

*This body will soon be consigned to the earth. Slowly it will decompose, and in a few months, it will be reduced to nothing—just a pile of bones, that's all. And yet when he was alive, he was not just a body with a physiological process that kept him going: there was more to him. There were his thoughts, his beliefs, his aspirations, his ideals. Now, those are gone.*

Her father, she remembered, wanted to take Warissah to the Natural History Museum in Port Louis the following month, and had planned to visit his cousin in Australia at the end of the year. That too wouldn't happen.

Humeirah retired to the adjoining room so that the men could begin the rituals. She badly wanted to be on her own: the hugging, shaking of hands, nodding, touching, and acknowledging were getting to her, as well as the civilities and hackneyed statements.

Zeba stepped into the room and closed the door. "Why are you here, Humeirah? Everyone wants to meet you."

Humeirah looked up, wondering if she could tell her how she felt.

"I don't feel like it, Zeba," she said, giving in to the inner voice. "It's tiring. They are just pouring in one after another and saying the same thing. I want to be alone."

"Oh, please, Humeirah, this is your father's funeral. For once, why can't you stop acting strange and do what everyone does?"

Humeirah looked down.

"Go out, Humeirah. Go and meet everyone. They want to see you."

***

Humeirah stood in a corner of the hall where everyone had gathered. Fatima was nearby and still engaged in gossip with Sarah.

"Yes, of course he cheats..." she whispered, not realising that Humeirah was within earshot. "Don't you know last month...Sana...she...divorcee. You know, how easy those divorcees...desperate. They'll do anything. Something wild...between them it seems. Humeirah doesn't know. Why do you think Sana likes him so much? She knows she can...rid of Humeirah easily...Money...Sana is...she will only go for the guy who can afford to..."

Humeirah stormed back into the room she had just walked out of, and Zeba, who had also overheard the exchange, followed her.

Humeirah sat in a chair with her head bowed.

"You shouldn't have gone out of the room," Zeba said.

"But you told me to!"

"I didn't. I just said that you shouldn't stay aloof from everyone at this time."

"But—Please, Zeba, let me be. I want to be alone."

An hour later, after being washed three times and wrapped in a *kafan*—a plain white inexpensive shroud consisting of three separate pieces—and perfumed with attar, Gibran's body was laid on a carpet at the entrance of the house. Men and women sat around once a "him", now an "it", repeating short verses from the Quran at the toss of date seeds to keep count. Some believed that reading verses at a funeral erased the sins of the deceased; others discounted it, although they went on to add that it was not a bad idea since it prevented people from indulging in gossip.

Humeirah stayed in the room, and after some time, overheard the raised voices of men reciting holy verses, imagining her father's body being lifted and carried out of the house to the cemetery in Bois Marchand—the one where Memons were buried.

After all the containment, retinue, or perhaps indifference, tears rolled down Humeirah's cheeks. But she knew better, and interpreted it as prompted by the gravity and severity of the Quran recitation that had culminated into a climax, unleashing the emotions she now felt.

That evening, men returning from the cemetery gathered to partake of the khunni ritual, where a mourner's meal, plainly cooked, of rice, dal, and vegetables, was served. By then, Humeirah had fallen asleep in the chair she had been in all along.

The next morning, she would wake up to an empty house—except for Kulssum who would be standing at the door, sad and forlorn, asking if someone could guide her because she didn't know where to go and what to do.

II

## -The Albatross-

Humeirah: "Who was Freud?"
They: "A crazy psychologist who was a sexual pervert."
Humeirah: "And Hitler?"
They: "A dictator who killed Jews."
Humeirah: "What about Socrates?"
They: "Uhh...a thinker?"
Humeirah: "Alexander the Great?"
They: "An important warrior from the past?"

Humeirah's eyes welled up, but the toxins in her body that sought release were insufficient, so that the tears merely accumulated in her eye sockets and dried up. She was in the same chair by the bed that she sat in while reading a book, but this time, she appeared distracted. She was mulling over what it signified to have Sana in her life.

*I tried so hard to have him. Why did she get him instead of me? What does she do that makes him happy? I wish I could watch them together and find out. What does she have that I don't? Am I undesirable? Unattractive?*

*Am I supposed to hate Sana because she is sleeping with my husband? Probably. But the truth is that I don't blame her. I don't blame him either. There is an organic process beyond reason, and beyond the duty to do right over wrong, that is in operation. In the end, desire often trumps duty, even if we speak about moral values that bind society.*

*I just have to accept the truth that I couldn't make it work.*

Tears filled her eyes again, and once more they dried up. Despite her attempts at rationalising, it was not human to be objective, to rationalise, to be so disconnected.

*Why do I deny the truth to myself? What am I trying to show?*

*That I am strong? I am not. I am angry and in pain.*

*Why couldn't it be me? I am here. I have always been here.*

Shanthi opened the door, saw Humeirah sitting idly with a book that wasn't being read, and shook her head. Earlier that day, she had told Vijay: "These storybooks that Humeirah reads are so pointless. What will she gain by reading? Stories are for children like Warissah."

Vijay had retorted: "Everyone has a passion, Shanthi, and Humeirah's is to read books, so let her be."

"There's a guest downstairs," Shanthi now told Humeirah. "I think it's the same person who came for the first time to the last houseparty. He says his name is Saahil or Aadil or something."

Humeirah looked up blankly at Shanthi. The name didn't register, and it was too much of an effort to figure it out.

Throughout the week, following Gibran's death, friends and relatives had poured in to pay their condolences, and Humeirah had kept away from everyone so that Haider had had to receive them on his own. But this time, since he was not in, Shanthi had had no choice but to call on Humeirah.

"Where's Haider?"

"Misyer Haider's out," replied Shanthi. Humeirah's thoughts flew to Sana, wondering whether Shanthi knew. After the latter left the room, she slipped out of her negligee and into a shalwar khameez. Stepping into the sitting room, she dreaded the courage and energy she would have to gather to come up with the usual pleasantries. But seated in one of the sofas, leafing through the pages of a magazine from the coffee table, was a man she recognised and who relieved her instantly of her fear.

Her exchanges with Saabir at Hannah's birthday party had been memorable and she had often revisited them in thought. He was the first person she had come across in her life who made her feel that she was safe, and could open her heart and speak to without being judged. She remembered that on that first meeting he had talked about a book he wanted to publish—or already published—she wasn't sure. She had wanted to ask him about it, but they ended up talking about so much else. Later, at the house party Haider had hosted, she had not had a chance to speak to him because the evening had ended on a sour note.

And although not a reason to like him any less, since she was prone to identifying idiosyncrasies in everyone, including people she liked and disliked, sometimes she recalled how he spoke pompously, and reminded her of Mr. Collins in *Pride and Prejudice*.

"Hello, Humeirah. How are you? I'm sorry for your loss," he said, standing up. "I couldn't attend the funeral. I was away in the UK to conclude a deal for my book."

Humeirah nodded, took a seat opposite his, and with her head bent, fiddled with her hands and remained silent.

"How are you feeling?"

"I'm all right, Saabir, thanks for asking."

"No, honestly. How are you holding up?"

It was the tone.

She looked up at the man she barely knew, but who—

"I wasn't very close to my father, Saabir. That's the truth. Maybe it hasn't sunk in. There are other matters on my mind, and I am trying to deal with them."

"Is it something you would like to talk about?"

Humeirah looked at him intently. Should she?

"No," said the little voice.

"It's all right, Saabir, thank you. I think I can handle it. Can we please talk about something else?"

Saabir smiled at her, but the silence that followed was awkward.

"You once asked about the book I published."

Humeirah nodded.

"Well, judging by the little I have seen of you, I think it will interest you. The theme is similar to the one in Baudelaire's poem *The Albatross*. Do you know it?"

Finally, a glimmer in her eyes.

"Yes, I do. Tell me more."

"I write about the disconnection that people feel when they have the mind and soul of an artist; mind you, an *artist* in the larger sense of the word, not just the artist who writes, sings, or paints."

"I know what you mean. *The Portrait of the Artist as a Young Man*. That's where I realised that. Having the soul of an artist is beyond what is produced as a result."

"Yes. Like *The Albatross*. Remember how the albatross is described as a magnificent bird when it is in its natural element in the sky, flapping its majestic wings over the sham and drudgery of mankind? Then, Baudelaire recounts how the same bird's wings turn into a curse as it lands on the ship's deck and tries to move, its wings getting in the way, while the sailors, the common folk, who look on, hurl stones at it in mockery."

"I've thought about it," said Humeirah, "When I first read the poem, I was marked by the idea. Later I realised that it was appealing to many precisely because it called out to our instinctive desire to be unique. But when in one's bubble, isn't that a false notion or romantic hope?"

Saabir paused contemplatively.

"You have a point, Humeirah. The poem's universality lies in appealing to our desire to be deemed unique. But you can't deny that it also captures the feeling of dissonance and disconnection many of us feel from the people who surround us. We end up being in the minority because of how we feel, and since this world revolves around numbers who give their consent as well as withhold it, we are the ones, however sound our thought or opinion, who turn into its victims."

The little girl behind the screen took a step forward, but as usual, only on tiptoe.

"So how do you cope with your differences, your isolation?" she asked.

"I surround myself with like-minded people."

"But Saabir, where are they? You are the first person I have met whom I have been able to connect with in this way."

"Yes, it's rare to come across someone you have a connection with. That's why when you do, you must latch on to him or her. I have come across only a handful of people whom I feel I share a connection with."

"Maybe I need your luck."

"Don't worry, Humeirah, it will happen sooner or later. I realised that the more I embraced my differences, the easier it became to draw such people to myself."

"I understand, but the only resistance I have to the *idea* of surrounding myself with like-minded people is that it feels cowardly and is such a convenient getaway. Isn't the engagement with difference important? It's among like-minded people that there is a surplus of dogma. Surely there must be a way of being part of the crowd while still being distant from it?"

"If it's what you are trying to do, Humeirah, my question is, are you coping?"

"Ye... No. It's hard. Nobody understands me. They think I am complicated, that I think too much."

"Then do you want to remain in this state, constantly exposed to people who challenge your belief in yourself, and destroy your self-esteem?"

"But this is unrealistic. You speak as if you know of a state of nirvana—of perfection—where one is content being surrounded by people who are in harmony with who you are. But how impossible! First, it's impossible to be happy or content, or just about anything, *all* the time. Just a romantic and unrealistic hope that takes you nowhere. Second, I don't see how I will find the people you mention who will be closer to who I am. Third, moving out of this circle of people won't necessarily bring me happiness, Saabir. At least, I don't think so. I get the feeling everyone who is slightly different, slightly a misfit, ends up reconciling himself or herself to living an atomised existence. Is this really the solution to all our cries for individualism? And then, I just can't imagine a world different from the one I have always known."

"No, there isn't absolute bliss anywhere in the world. But what you know is only *a* world. I don't wish to sound patronising, Humeirah, but you haven't really seen much. Our island's insularity affects us in many more ways than we imagine. Still, it is my belief that if you surround yourself with people who are closer to you in spirit, you will be better equipped to cope with life's ups and downs. And they *are* here. You just haven't left the cocoon you've always known. Take Virginia Woolf. Do you know that her artistic ingenuity, the novel style of her writing, is attributed to the fact that she was surrounded by people who encouraged her to explore her talent, and by that, I mean that which was odd, quirky and intense about her?"

"It sounds so easy when you put it this way. Breaking away from my reality, the family I have grown up with, the society that has moulded me into who I am, is like reordering everything I know about myself. I don't even know where to start, or how to get there."

"It's hard work indeed, but most people who don't get out are trapped, fail to realise the ramifications, and end up complaining all their lives about being misfits. It's easier *not* to fight, Humeirah; to accept what one has and go along with it. It's easier to be lazy."

"Reconstructing a narrative, Saabir, making new laws from scratch for oneself may sound very inspiring, but where I am right now, I am caught up with the nitty-gritty details of life. I don't think I have what it takes to break free. I would love to be free; to focus on the bigger things of life. It's as though my thoughts are muffled in this small space. Try as I might, I can't push my thinking beyond certain limits because the environment is just not right. I fear surprising myself with thoughts that are utterly radical and would never be accepted by the society I am in. It's been this way all along. Every time I managed to push thinking to another level, and started believing in something different, people noticed and called me weird, eccentric...even mad. I am caught in a state of conflict where, on one hand, I struggle to fit in, and on the other, fight to let my thoughts take me where they want to go. I'm not sure what to make of it."

"I understand, but, ultimately, it's your choice. I am just telling you that there is someone out there who feels the same way as you do; that you are not alone; that there is even a way out if you are willing to risk it."

"How did you get the freedom?"

"I too had to break free, Humeirah. When the time is right, I will tell you my story. For now, I just want to say that you have more hurdles to overcome because you are a woman, and doubly so, because you were brought up in a traditional and orthodox setting. My surroundings were different, and still, I too had to put up a fight despite being a male member of this society, and by that token, privileged, and despite the relatively lax norms compared to yours."

Shanthi stepped into the room. Noting that the tray she had brought in earlier with tea and samosas was untouched, she asked Saabir if he needed anything else.

The truth was that Humeirah and Saabir hadn't noticed her walk in, then and now—both times, clearly peeved.

Saabir left the house with a heavy heart that day. He felt he had failed to communicate in a meaningful way with Humeirah.

Sometimes the time was not propitious for a thought, a feeling, a realisation—however reasonable, sensible and necessary; no matter how many times reiterated or acknowledged—to be adhered to or digested by the one who was badly in need of it. And in Humeirah's failure to understand what Saabir meant by his entreaty to her to leave, this seemed most likely the reason.

# III

## -Venus in Furs-

Ralph Waldo Emerson: "When Nature has work to be done, she creates a genius to do it."
Humeirah: "But man interferes and beheads him."


Everyone knew that Sana was a head-turner. Oozing sensuousness, she could awaken the dormant—even dead—monster of desire in any man. Conscious of the power she had over the opposite sex, she would look into a man's eyes, seize his gaze, and guide the movement of his pupils in synchrony with hers till he was at her mercy.

In time, weary of these games, Sana had sought to pacify the rapturous and deviant monster in her and did so by giving in to the bond of matrimony.

"I wish to be stable and consistent," she told herself, and so she was.

It took four months for her to realise that she had made a mistake. Bridling something inherently wild and uncontrollable could never truly tame it. By then however, it was not easy to get rid of a husband who was awed by the power she had over him and other men, although he did not care to admit it.

When she returned to her erstwhile habits and seduced someone into sleeping with her, to her surprise, he worshipped and submitted himself to her and did not utter a word to show either consternation or disapprobation.

Sana was resilient and sought to augment the tempo and cycle of abuses, day and night directing vituperative remarks at him, expecting him to punish her with the silent treatment and even sulk and lash out for having transgressed limits of decency. Instead, he returned silence and submission, and when Sana discerned the dull expression of subservience impressed on his face, she pushed the humiliation further by belittling him in front of friends and relatives, shouting orders, using coarse invectives, treating him as obtuse, worthless, good-for-nothing, to no avail.

He remained quiet, apologised, and blamed himself for annoying and angering his clever and beautiful wife. Her surprise knew no bounds. She could not believe that she had settled for someone so cowardly and regretted her decision to marry him. She deserved better.

In recovering from the poison of her venom—quickly done—he waited for every opportunity to be at her service.

When she was in the shower, he would put a hold on his activities, select a shalwar khameez from the wardrobe, lay it out with care on the bed, and place matching shoes, jewellery and other accessories beside it, waiting for her at the edge of the bed as she stepped out in her bathrobe.

Often, she would voice her dissatisfaction with his selections and manifest it in a number of unpleasant ways, including commenting on his lack of exposure to the world. It was not untrue. Unlike many members of the Memon community, Sana's husband had not ventured elsewhere than Rodrigues Island. She compared him to their mutual first cousin Ayn who had migrated to England with his wife and two children. Ayn had said that if Memons were inherently travellers who had been perpetually displaced, first abandoning their Hindu families after converting to Islam in the fifteenth century, and later, leaving India to settle in Mauritius and other parts of the world, then he had to continue the trend by moving somewhere better.

Sana's husband responded to her taunts by hanging his head and apologising, promising to inquire about migrating to Canada or Australia. Then, in regaining his composure, he would hurry to look for something more pleasing to her taste for her to wear that evening. Throughout the time, he would cling to the thought that she could not live without him, obsessed by the memory of the few times she had been delighted by his selections.

Time went by and Sana grew impatient and bored, and more than ever, missed the thrill of the chase. In doubling her efforts to seduce men and take them back to her house, she began entertaining them in his presence. At first, her men-trophies were puzzled, but only for a while, her indifference compelling them to count him as negligible. They just wanted him out of the way, and it didn't take much for it to happen. Sana's husband ignored the provocation at first. In time however, he came to terms with what was happening and started by giving her the silent treatment.

"Finally!" she thought.

But days went by, and nothing changed; instead, he began to show more signs of being weakened.

One day, he came up to her, took her in his arms and said that he had thought about it, and realised that he had it in him to forgive her, and was willing to make it work despite her flaws, despite everything.

Sana was shocked; she wanted to be punished, not forgiven. And who was he to believe he was in control and say such awful things to her?

But he wasn't done. He told her that her success with men had convinced him further that he was the luckiest man alive to have her as his wife, since she slept with him and only him, while her relationships with them were fleeting and insubstantial.

She watched and listened to him. "What an apt and convenient justification," she remarked to herself. "What an apt coping mechanism."

After that, the door to their bedroom remained shut. Many a time, he knocked, pleading to be let in; pleading that he didn't mind the hideous beast that commanded her moves; pleading that he was eager to care for it, feed it and tend to its needs, if that's what it took for her to accept him back.

Finally, Sana made up her mind to leave their conjugal home. Her husband sobbed and begged, summoning his friends and then hers, detailing his life story and then hers, so that they could understand how much he needed her and how much he thought she did.

"What a big mistake she is making," he told her and them, "leaving someone who truly loves her for who she is."

While she dismissed him, they listened, empathised and promised that they would speak to her at the first given opportunity. He was relieved; he hoped for the best.

But they never did. All they wished was to avoid dealing with anything difficult, including negativity, conflict, and every form of discomfort which would accrue if they interfered with matters that didn't concern them. And because they weren't sufficiently self-aware to acknowledge this, they justified (or disguised) their apathy by telling one another as well as themselves that Nature had her own way of restoring equilibrium, so that time would inevitably reveal solutions to Sana and her husband's predicament.

Once divorced, Sana embarked on a different challenge, since, for all intents and purposes, she was now one of the few divorcees in a close-knit community of one thousand, where all forms of marital separation were rare and thus frowned upon; frowned upon and thus rare. If inevitable, a separation would take place under the conjugal roof, discreetly, with only the few knowing of it, leading to the silent implosion of the family unit over time. In such an instance, one would be doomed to live for the rest of one's life with a partner who had effortlessly turned into a pebble in the shoe.

If Sana was not the woman she was, she would have feared being mistreated and shown disrespect to by men, women and children since a divorcee was deemed an easy catch. A divorcee had developed a taste for intimacy, it was believed, so that who went in and out made no difference because the door had been broken down. Men thus swarmed around her, drooling, each impatient to have a turn.

But Sana knew better and wished to maintain standards. She did not want to be an ordinary divorcee—and wasn't. Every time she met someone new, she interviewed him, assessed what she could get out of the liaison, and analysed the damage that could arise from an association as well as the extent of his prejudice towards her.

By the time she met Haider at Hannah's birthday party, she had been embroiled in a few affairs, most of them brief. Every lover she had entangled herself with had craved for more even if he was in a relationship, ready to give everything up and leave his partner to be with her. One or two went ahead and deserted their conjugal home, only to end up in the arms of a woman no longer willing to take it further.

Haider fitted the archetype of the partner she settled with for a while before moving on to another. His hunger for power and money gave him the aplomb that made him stand out— just the aphrodisiac she needed.

But Haider was more difficult to weaken and subjugate than she had imagined. Still, she was resilient, confident that it was a matter of time. For now, as in all her liaisons, she would enjoy the offerings of luxury that he would shower on her—a fair exchange, she thought, for the time devoted to a lover.

What she didn't know was that Haider too looked upon his gifts and bounties to her as barter. He was paying to be seen with a beautiful woman, and pitied Sana for not knowing any better.

Sana's plan came to fruition. Haider realised he wanted more. He had never come across a woman—especially a Memon—who exerted such an effect on others in spite of her morally objectionable character. Owning a woman like her, he reasoned, and appearing in parties and other functions beside her could benefit him both, socially and professionally.

But he knew the rules of the game. He showed more resistance to her charms than he ordinarily would. Later, he told her that he was devising plans to get rid of Humeirah-.

By then however, Sana was not in love with him. For a short while, she had thought she was and even *wanted* to be, but when she realised how she had slowly relinquished her autonomy, she convinced herself that this was like every other game. What she really wished for, she told herself, was to watch the serene and majestic walk of the King of the Jungle turn into the frenzied pace of the rodent, desperate for the meagre offerings thrown at him—that's all.

At first, Haider and Sana met occasionally and openly. Then the meetings grew more regular and erotic as they opted for isolated surroundings. In their lovemaking sessions, she treated him like an accessory for her own pleasure, guiding his moves and giving him detailed instructions, which he obeyed, wanting more than anything to give her what she wanted. In turn, he expected her to tend to his cravings, which she did but only reservedly when it came to what she deemed beneath her.

Sana recognised the power Haider had over her despite her resistance, but made sure not to reveal it to him for fear that it would go to his head. And then, she didn't want it to be difficult when she would eventually walk out. As for Haider, he too did not reveal how besotted he was by her, since it would be an overt sign of weakness. The games they played ended up prolonging the relationship, and soon, it was the longest Sana remembered being in.

Word about their Sana and Haider's affair spread among friends and relatives. With impatience, they waited for him to make an official announcement that he was going to leave Humeirah and marry Sana, but it never happened.

Many wondered whether Humeirah knew about her husband's affair. Some were sad that her husband was betraying her; others said that she deserved it. But everyone was unanimous in claiming that it was only human that the unhappy and lonely Haider had ended up with just-any-other-woman, a divorcee, as Sana.

Then, out of the blue, without conscious effort, they underwent a change of mind, reversing Sana's reputation from that of a promiscuous woman—a cheap-nothing—to a noble woman of sublime beauty who promised everything a man could want to be happy.

IV

# -Through the Eyes of the Innocent-

"Friendship: The story of betrayal." The little voice in Humeirah's head

At ten o'clock in the evening, in one of the bedrooms of Haider's house, a young girl lay in bed on the verge of falling asleep. On her insistence, a doll had been placed beside her.

In the dim room, Dolly's wide eyes were glued to the ceiling, while Warissah's narrowed into slits. Shanthi stood over her, caressing her hair, waiting for the meagre openings to disappear before slipping out.

"Ti, what happened to Nana?"

Warissah raised the question for the first time. The day her grandfather died, Vijay had driven her to his house without saying a word. Nobody had explained the purpose of the visit so she had assumed that it was one of those days she would have to stay over for the night.

As they neared the house, she sat up straight to get a better look outside. Cars—an unusual number, big and small, long and short, red, black, blue, and white, and one that was marshmallow pink—were lined up on either side of the street. Nana was surely throwing a party. Questions popped up in her mind: would they stay over for the night too?

But there weren't enough beds.

Would they have dinner with him at the table the way she did?

But there weren't enough chairs.

Would Nana give them chocolates as he did after dinner?

When Warissah stepped into the house, despite the crowd, everyone was quiet. She wondered why almost everyone, either seated or standing, bowed their heads and only spoke in whispers and hushed tones. No one said the usual Assalamualaikum to one another, and when she did, it was neither acknowledged nor answered.

Nana was in his room, she was told, and concluded that he was sleeping. How odd. Why didn't he wake up? He always said that it was rude to be asleep when someone was visiting. She also noticed that a few men kept going in and out of his room. Wouldn't it disturb him? Nana could get angry.

That day however, she had not been present when her grandfather's body was carried out since Vijay had dropped her home before the rituals for the burial began. For the rest of the week, she overheard guests who came to visit her parents, mention him, and speak as if he would never come back—something was not normal.

"Ti, what happened to Nana?" repeated Warissah. Shanthi was fumbling for the right words.

"He has gone away, Warissah."

"Where?"

"To Heaven."

"Where is that?"

"Heaven is a place far away from here. When people die, they go to Heaven."

"He won't come back?"

"No..."

"Why do people go away?"

"Because God calls them."

"Why?"

Shanthi pondered over this. "Because God likes them so much that he calls them to stay with Him."

"When will Nana come back?"

"Nana won't come back, Warissah."

"Why?"

"Because God likes him a lot and God will keep him forever."

"When can I see Nana?"

"Not soon, Warissah. Now, get some sleep."

"I want to see Nana."

Warissah was about to burst into tears. Shanthi wondered how she could tell Warissah that she would no longer spend the night at his place, sit at the table with him, or even see him. Something however interrupted that.

Shanthi and Warissah overheard Humeirah and Haider's raised voices in the adjoining room.

"went away..... why not me?....Sana had..." shouted Humeirah in despair and an uproar followed. "...bitch ...don't you..." followed, and the sound of furniture being pushed, something falling with a crash, more cries of despair from Humeirah, and finally, silence.

Shanthi and Warissah were both straining their ears, trying to discern the reason for the commotion.

There was an abrupt noise again, and another cry of distress.

Warissah sprang to her knees, grabbed Dolly, and ran out of her bedroom into the adjoining one where her parents were. Shanthi followed her meekly, stopping outside the door, keeping a distance from the scene.

Humeirah was on the floor. Haider was sitting on top of her with her legs pinned between his, and both shouting at each other; one fiercely, the other pleadingly.

"Stop. Please stop. Please don't fight," cried Warissah, covering her ears. She barely managed to cover her left ear because of Dolly.

Haider and Humeirah didn't seem to notice her.

"Why don't you shut your mouth? So what if I see her? It's none of your business. What good are you anyway? I should never have married you. You are a mad crazy bitch."

Humeirah was trying to express herself in between sobs. Haider stood up and stormed out of the room, ignoring Warissah and Shanthi. Warissah rushed to her mother, leaned over her, and held her head against her own, kissing her forehead. "Why did this happen? Mummy, please don't cry."

Humeirah hugged her daughter, half-leaning against the floor and half-resting her weakened body in a lap that felt soft, delicate and vulnerable. A contrast to the strong and tough figure that had wrested control of her body. She tried to get a hold of herself. It was unfair on her daughter to endure this.

Earlier, she had tried to convince herself not to bring up the matter she wanted to broach with Haider, suspecting how it would end. In the end, torn between the desire for peace and the need to sort out their differences, she had given in.

As for Warissah, in her world where words, concepts and thought processes were yet unclear, after enduring such scenarios, she was unsure who to love and who to resent. It was impossible to love her parents, but it was also impossible to resent them.

Sometimes she resented her mother because it was clear that she had started the quarrels; at other times she eyed her father with disdain for what he would have done to her mother.

In her young and tender years, with conflict raging and tearing her apart, little Warissah was getting acquainted with the controversies of life that would gradually mould and chisel the predilections of her heart and mind.

V

# -Our Legacy to Mankind-

"What will I leave behind for mankind? Warissah?" Humeirah

Somewhere far away, the first rays of sunlight appeared on the horizon as the glimmering disc glided out of the sea and moved all the way up into the sky, brightening the world, raising its temperature, beckoning animals and human beings out of their burrows, summoning petals to display their impudicity.

Humeirah was in bed, comforted by the warmth of the room as the rays of sunlight filtered through sheer curtains that fluttered with the light breeze. After opening her eyes, she liked to stay in bed, plan how she would spend the day, where she would go, what she would read, or mull over the dream she had had—that is, if she could remember.

Today, she was jotting down her thoughts in her diary. She could hear the birds, but resisted going out. Shanthi had voiced her irritation that Humeirah had taken to feeding them—something she had begun to enjoy, watching them fly down one by one from the nearby litchi tree to peck raw rice. It marked her that the birds seemed less and less fearful every time another descended, when they had remained concealed in the tree at the beginning, observing her from afar.

At a bookstore in Vacoas, Humeirah had bought a book about birds, and could now identify village weavers, streaky-headed seedeaters, common mynahs, common waxbills, Mauritius fodies, red-whiskered bulbuls, house sparrows, zebra doves and malagasy turtle doves, among others, noting the little things that differentiated them from one another. The village weaver, she wrote in her diary, because of its comparable height, extended its feet to bend over and peck, while the common waxbill, with a deep red-orange hue around its eyes, seemed to don a pair of bright sporty shades. She contemplated writing a poem about them. In charcoal, she sketched them perched on the electric wires outside the gate, and coloured them.

Next, Humeirah hoped to distinguish them through the sounds they made, but the aspiration was short-lived. Shanthi complained that "ban zoizo pe fer malang." Because of their droppings, she now had the added chore of filling buckets of water daily to clean the backyard.

It didn't cross her mind to ask Humeirah to handle it on her behalf, nor did the latter suggest it, knowing that this was one more means through which Shanthi was trying to assert her dominion. She would make sure to have it her way.

Humeirah closed her diary and peered at the bedside table. A book with a black cover read: *The Metamorphosis*. She reached out for it, turned to the first page, read a few lines and stopped.

*More than a century ago, a man took up a pen and wrote the words I am reading. He left behind what was most intimate, because while writing, he took pauses to sleep, eat, relieve himself, speak in between to his loved ones, laugh, cry....think...imagine....believe...hope.*

*And all these feelings, as well as emotions and states-of-being influenced the larger project he was working on, so that they are now immortalised in the interstices of his words.*

*What a marvellous way of leaving something behind.*
Absent-mindedly, she leafed through a few more pages.
*What will I leave behind? Warissah? Yes. Another woman, another living being, who will do what everybody else does.*
Then, she turned the pages in the opposite direction and read:

Franz Kafka (1883-1924) was a German-language author of short stories and novels and is regarded as one of the most renowned writers of the 20th century. Kafka was born to middle-class Jewish parents in Prague, Bohemia, then part of the Austro-Hungarian Empire. During his lifetime, he published only a few short stories. He completed the novella *The Metamorphosis*, but never any of his full-length novels. Kafka left his published and unpublished work to his friend and also his literary executor with explicit instructions that it should be destroyed on his death. Kafka wrote: "Dearest Max, my last request: Everything I leave behind me...in the way of diaries, manuscripts, letters, sketches, and so on are to be burned, unread." His executor however decided to ignore this request and went on to publish them.

Kafka's childhood was fraught with difficulties. In a letter to his father he—

Humeirah averted her eyes.
*Kafka—the rightful owner of his work—had no control over what ought to have been his. Once he put down his pen, he could not claim his own work back; it belonged to the world and the world went on to do what it wished.*
*How helpless he would have felt had he known what happened after his death.*
Humeirah's thoughts went to Warissah.
*However hard I'd try, I knew that I would never have a hold over her. Her life could turn out to be good or end up a complete wreck.*
A vision of Warissah flashed before her eyes; of her holding Dolly, tending to her, combing her hair with a plastic comb, taking care to pick clothes for their outings, displaying an air of seriousness in fulfilling the tasks and assuming the role. Then, the image of the world crowded with the people Humeirah knew emerged.
How she wished she could cover her daughter with a sheet that had magical powers and made her invisible.
How she wished she could prevent the inevitable transformation her daughter was bound to undergo.
Humeirah glanced at the far end of the room.
In the early days of her marriage, she had requested for a set of shelves for her bedroom. With a displeased grunt, Haider had conceded, so that Shanthi's son Raj had walked in with his tools and fixed them. It was a simple setup, nondescript and lacking aesthetic appeal.
Nobody in Humeirah's surroundings would or could understand the pleasure she derived lying on her back, scanning her book collection.
*How I wish Warissah could read these.*
*I may not be the master of my environment, but these books have been the light that have made the path less obscure when I was lost.*

*These books made a parody of the stereotypes and archetypes of people I began to discern in my surroundings, and it became easier to be with myself.*

*These books have jolted me out of my stifling and monotonous environment, and exposed me to other worlds, as well as to the intricacies of other minds. I have lived, existed and breathed through them and they have added colour to my life.*

*These books have exposed me to the best and worst emotions, so that I now have a sounder appreciation of how much time and energy certain matters should be given over others. I may not have completely mastered that, but I am conscious of its virtue.*

*Yes, these books have exposed me to almost the entire scale of emotions and have taught me how to respond measuredly to people and to situations. They have given me answers that I looked for from people and never found.*

*These books have given me the solace and confidence to dare to think differently.*

*Yes, sometimes I struggle with the fact that my opinions about so much aren't well formed, so that whenever I read an author or philosopher, I find myself adopting his or her stance, and later, on reading another with a contrary view, end up agreeing with him or her too.*

*But maybe that's the whole point. Maybe with time and exposure, I will have firmer opinions—my own opinions.*

*But is the world I live in right now giving me the exposure I need?*

Divided into two sections—read and unread—and each organised in order of genre and then height, there were a hundred or more books collected over the years. A modest number, but in light of what they represented to the great markings of history, Humeirah knew their worth to be unquestionable.

She peered at her books in the faint light of the morning sun.

*I was a whole being like everyone else. I had my own thoughts and ideas that had gained permanence and couldn't be jostled around: they were capped and retained within the person I was. Even when I was exposed to other minds, I retained the stagnancy. My fixed thoughts, notions, and impressions became the ultimate standard of measuring others and their worth, so that I was prejudiced and judgmental. I was never the overflowing fountain, but the cistern that was stagnant. I craved to be continuous and to see life through the eyes of others; to melt into their vision and be part of something bigger and greater. But these books...these books have opened a whole new world for me.*

*When I read, I abandon my capped self: I become part of a greater whole. Merging. Being less lonely—that's what these books do. They make life more bearable.*

A smile of contentment played on Humeirah's lips as she closed the book with care, placed it on the bedside table and leaned back. After a long time, she was content to be who she was.

# VI

## -Intimacies-

"When a mouse laughs at the cat, he knows that a hole is nearby." Chinese proverb
Humeirah: "When a mouse laughs at the cat, the cat mistook herself for a cat."

The door to Humeirah's bedroom creaked and woke her up. It was late in the night, and she could discern outlines of objects in the room—including Haider's silhouette as he prowled up to her bed. She imagined his puffy eyes at that hour.

There was nothing unusual about the intrusion. When he sneaked in at this hour, she knew that it wasn't to snuggle up to her, or utter words of love and comfort—no. Haider had a craving.

Humeirah had tried to discern a pattern in his trespasses so that they would not be unexpected. She wanted to know, so that when it happened, she could take the torment in her stride. But there was no science to it, and every time he intruded into her world, it was unexpected and the anguish never ceased. It was on a similar night, long ago, that Warissah had been conceived.

Haider guessed that she might be awakened by his presence in the room, but still chose to sneak in surreptitiously. Something kept him from claiming it too openly—call it guilt—although he believed it his right to be here and to be gratified. In the end, it fostered a strain in the air that both parties now felt.

Standing over Humeirah's curled up body that faced the other side, he pulled off his creased T-shirt and undid the string that held his baggy shorts. Then, he slipped into the bed and poked her arm twice. She turned around and lay flat, facing the ceiling, and he began undressing her in an act that lacked sensuality, manoeuvring his way to place her body parts in the right position.

Once it was done, he leaned back, paused, and cast a final glance at her body, his eyes brimming with satisfaction. Then he lunged forward to tackle the final step. Sometimes if her arm or leg came in the way, he shoved it aside as if it was an external intrusion—a dead leaf that had fallen out of nowhere and settled on the canvas of wet paint he had been working on.

Haider moved on top of Humeirah. She stared at him. She could see him more clearly now. His eyes were shut and the wrinkles that appeared around them showed how hard he was trying to focus. His naked body grazed hers in vertical rhythms as he held his breath, concentrating so hard that his body stiffened.

Humeirah turned away, steadying her view of the bookshelf, trying to discern the titles to distract herself. Her mind wouldn't shut down.

*It's the look on his face. I can't stand it.*

*He could well be seated over a toilet bowl, constipated.*

She wondered what this scene would look like to a bystander and was almost humoured, reminded of the times she had seen animals copulating—a big dog on another dog, a big horse on another horse.

Haider was oblivious to the person instrumental in giving him pleasure, and avoided looking in her eyes and at her body. In the early days, Humeirah had wondered why. Was she ugly? Repulsive? Maybe he was trying to focus on gaining pleasure, or maybe he didn't want to look into her expressionless eyes.

While Haider was inside her, Humeirah remembered the exercise of syllogistic reasoning she had learned in school:

First premise: Humeirah ought to feel good when a man is inside her.

Second premise: Haider is a man.

Conclusion: Therefore, Humeirah ought to feel good when Haider is inside her.

It didn't make sense. This didn't feel good at all.

However daunting these moments, from the beginning, she had yearned for physical contact. It made her feel needed and desirable and it was all the intimacy she had in the relationship.

Later, when she understood that he didn't love her and that she was merely a vent for his lust, she wanted him to do his thing and leave.

That night however, while he was inside her, there was a change: images of Sana flashed through her mind.

*Argh. It hurts.*

Humeirah shifted her thoughts back to what was on her mind. Haider was taking a long time to climax—she wanted to push him away but feared his reaction.

At that moment, she realised that sex could be a means for her to exert control over him—there could be revenge in the act of giving. She had flashes of the image of a rich passer-by dropping a coin in the lap of a beggar, knowing that the latter would not be able to return the kindness. She too wanted to feel like that, since in any case, she didn't feel anything during their sexual intimacies.

Haider's body entered a series of convulsions until he had his fill. From the corner of her eye, Humeirah could still see his face. An image formed in her mind—of him finally squeezing out a hardened stool.

Humeirah braced herself and stared into his eyes with calm indifference. He saw it and briefly, his confidence plummeted. Haider who at other such times was proud and confident could no longer meet her eyes.

But soon enough, he restored his mien, put on his shorts and lay next to her, propped up against the pillows like the sultan of a majestic kingdom. Then for the first time, she saw him take out a cigarette from one of his pockets and light it. She felt irrelevant.

She looked at him: he had a distant look of pleasure as he drew on his cigarette and blew out thick draughts. The inhaling-exhaling was the final act. What she felt was of no importance to him. Henceforth, Humeirah lost all feeling of power. She was wrong; I was wrong—he was always in control.

After Haider finished his cigarette, he walked out of his wife's bedroom and closed the door. Not a word had been exchanged.

Humeirah slipped on her clothes, lay in bed and stared at the ceiling, not wanting to give the incident further thought, for fear of cringing—cringing yet again.

*It's time for change.*
She focused on the hope it evoked to forget the bitter experience.

## VII

## -A Cocoon within a Cocoon-

"What if I get rid of things about me that irritate everyone, only to find that they are cherished by those who matter?" Humeirah

Oral historians, young and old, some attentive to detail, others prone to exaggeration—but all self-proclaimed—abounded among the Memons. They discussed events that had occurred in the recent century, momentous to the fate of individuals, families, and the community at large, comprising details of when the Memons arrived in Mauritius from Kutch, the nature of the trade they were involved in, among others.

After hearing these accounts, the difference between these moments—dear for the lack of recorded history—and more universally known historical markings, of say, King Harold being defeated by William the Conqueror at the Battle of Hastings in 1066, became blurred. One came to discern—and hence demystify—the magic behind the making of history, and with it, came the realisation of the fine line between fact and fiction.

Certainly, there were events, more specific and of doubtless consequence, such as the sinking of a ship (some said it was called *Sikandar*; others disputed it) in April 1892 at the Port Louis Harbour during the passage of an intense tropical cyclone, that among others, had carried a few Memons on a journey to India. Descendants of those who had dropped relatives and witnessed the ship sink recounted the tragedy with zest and conviction, one recounting how his great-great grandfather had had a dream on the eve, and tried to stop his brother from boarding the ship, but since these details were varied and often contradictory, they provoked a distrust of other more widely documented moments—they too, specific, of say, whether King Harold was really killed by an arrow in the eye.

***

Yusuf, one of Mr. Shah's six brothers, and Haider's most favourite uncle, was a revered member of the family, it being widely acknowledged that he was *un homme instruit et cultivé*, or that lin gagne gran ledikasyon. He was the first among his contemporaries to obtain a master's degree in Finance and Economics from a university in Pune. He owned books stacked in order of height on shelves extending from floor to ceiling against the three walls of his library; the neatness, he suggested, reflecting the methodical workings of his mind. The fourth was left bare for the door as well as a study table and chair carved out of high-quality Indonesian teakwood, that, for this and other reasons, remained untouched.

Yusuf bought one book every week after consulting newspaper advertisements, having adopted the practice since his mid-twenties. He was introduced as such, although he went on to intimate that he was collecting them and planned to read after retirement. For now, he had to do what everyone else did by tending to his family, working, making money and succeeding.

Everyone turned to him for advice on just about everything, including marriage proposals and decisions about sending children abroad for studies, more specifically, whether it was worth the money, as well as the most lucrative branch of education to enrol them into. Yusuf had wise pronouncements on every subject, one being that the cost of education abroad ought never exceed expected remunerations over a five-year-long period, post-graduation, otherwise it was not worth the while.

People also sought him out to acquaint themselves with political and financial ongoings in the country, and the details of its vacillating relationship with India because it affected everything, including investment-related decisions. Or still, how to deal with a pesky boss, colleague or relative, since he also understood the workings of the world, as daily and unfailingly, he perused local newspapers.

"Aftaab Alibokus? I don't know him," he told Faraaz, Haider's father, "but I knew an Alibokus long ago: Majeed."

Haider had invited the two brothers as well as a few other people to a last-minute tea party at his house. After the death of his father-in-law, people had phoned or dropped by to pay their condolences, but the numbers had naturally dwindled over time, leaving him restless and agitated, bereft of company and chatter. Organising last-minute tea parties was a way to compensate for the void.

Yusuf and Faraaz were going through the list of invitees to Kareem and Ambareen's wedding. It was a sensitive exercise. Should someone important be mistakenly excluded, it would be interpreted as intentional, causing bad blood and triggering a cycle of revenge so that the defaulter and his or her closest allies would be excluded from future events organised by the party taking offence.

"Aftaab must be related to Majeed Alibokus," Yusuf continued, "one of my old teachers at Islamic College. Maybe his son or nephew."

"But there are so many Alibokuses and they're not all related!" said Faraaz. "Their names are spelled in so many ways. I know of A l y b o k u s, A l l y b o k u s, A l l y b a c c u s, A l i b a c c u s."

"Actually," said Yusuf, "these names are all wrongly spelled. I can imagine what happened. When these Calcattias first came to Mauritius as indentured labourers, the Britons and French colonials noted their Urdu names wrongly. It should be A l i b a k s h—meaning, blessings of Ali. Just as Hossebaccus ought to be Hussein Baksh; or Mamodally, Mohammad Ali, or Ramatally, Rehmat Ali. Not like the Memons who came here as traders and had more bargaining power and asked that their names be spelled out correctly."

"Hmm, Papa used to say that too," said Faraaz. "But I'm not sure about how true that is, because most of the Memons who came here couldn't speak or write in English so they didn't have much of a say in how their names were spelled. Therefore, like the Calcattias, many ended up having names that were also—"

"Is it? Did Papa say that too? I don't remember that." Yusuf paused and peered reflectively at the floor and shook his head. "Poor Papa."

"Why do you say 'poor'?" said Faraaz.

"Obviously for all that he went through in his last days, in bed, dying a slow and painful death from TB."

"Our father was a happy and jolly man till the end."

"What do you mean? How can you say that? Papa suffered so much. He could never come to terms with how we—especially *you*—left him in Port Louis and moved our expanding families to Quatre Bornes and Floreal. He remained sore about it till the end."

"Faraaz, that's nonsense. You are younger than me, that's why you don't remember.

"By four years? Be reasonable. We were in our thirties when Papa passed away."

Yusuf and Faraaz argued about the state of mind of their dying father, an event that had occurred more than thirty years ago, until an awkward and angry silence set in and Faraaz stood up and walked away.

Later, Faraaz Shah would cross out *Mr. and Mrs. Yusuf Shah & Fly (4 pax)* from the invitation list. Yusuf and Faraaz's four siblings, after hearing reasoned and unreasoned arguments from both, would choose to adopt the ones embraced by the brother they were closer to, which in turn, would determine who among them would be present at Kareem and Ambareen's wedding.

***

Meanwhile, Anusha and Valesha were spending the weekend at the house, and were in the playroom with Warissah, and Shanthi was not her normal self. An aunt had passed away, and though distant in many respects, it dawned on her now how important she had been to the family's name and prestige.

"Kalooma was very kiltiver," she told Vijay, who was lending a helping hand with laying the table, preparing tea, and frying batches of beef samosas. "She spoke French all the time. When someone spoke Creole or Bhojpuri, she would only answer in French, so that very soon, everyone around her tried to do the same. She was such an influence! Maybe she didn't have as much wealth as these *gran dimoun* like Misyer Haider and his family, but you can say she was no different. Money is not everything."

Humeirah stepped into the sitting room after all the guests had arrived. When she noticed Saabir by himself in a corner, unhesitatingly, she walked up to him."

"*Pena haya,*" remarked a few.

"*Mank tarbiyat,*" said others.

Not far away, in a large cluster, men discussed erecting a new centre for Memons to congregate for daily prayers, one proposing to append a separate hall for weddings, Eid parties, khatams and milaads within the community. Among other things being debated were the funding of the project, and the observation was made that there was no need to contract the services of professionals outside the Memon community since all the experts were right here.

"I am tired of all this talk about Memons," Humeirah whispered to Saabir.

"You know," he said, "people outside the Memon or Surti Community, including many Calcattias, don't even know about us. I was speaking to a Franco-Mauritian writer, one of the most brilliant writers of the Indian Ocean, and when I asked whether he knew about us, he smiled, hesitated, and then said 'Are you referring to the Sunni-Surti divide?' I bet he meant Sunni-Shia divide, but of course, what I was talking about wasn't even close. I explained that the Sunni-Shia divide is belief-based, while the Memon-Surti-Calcattia one is founded on cultural differences hinging on places of origin, nothing else. But, Humeirah, let me tell you what I've observed: the Calcattias are coming up very fast. While the Memons have focused on founding and expanding businesses and making money, the Calcattias have gone on to concentrate on education. Do you know what is now being said by them about Memons? That they are mere shopkeepers!"

Humeirah listened to everything Saabir was saying, despite the subject. It was the clarity and insightfulness of his thought; the relevance of his speech. For the first time, she noted that his voice had a quality she could not put her finger on; something about how passionate and warm it was; how vivid and unpredictable, so that he was perpetually receptive and responsive to what was unfolding in his surroundings. What a contrast to the monotone of voices around her. For a while, she wondered whether she too possessed the quality, envying its possession, less its possessor.

Still, she wanted to direct him away from the subject. There was so much more to talk about, she thought, and here was a person offering the possibility.

"Saabir, tell me more, because I want to know. I too want to publish my writing one day. How do you know when a work is done? I can't imagine ever finishing something. I've tried, but I keep thinking it needs more work, more editing."

"A legitimate question, Humeirah. It's true that it's hard to deem a work as complete. Over the years, I've realised that, at least for me, it's when I don't want to make changes, irrespective of the state of mind I am in."

"What do you mean?"

"Well, sometimes you feel a certain way when you wake up, when you're about to sleep, when you're tired, or even when you're hungry. I try to read my work in all these states, and if it still makes sense and requires no emendation, then I know it's ready."

Humeirah was about to speak, but Shaheen appeared with Hannah in her arms, heaving a loud sigh as she merged into their cluster.

"I'm tired of these people," she said, "I need to leave this country. It's getting too small for me. Too many ti lespri here."

Neither Humeirah nor Saabir were keen on asking the question expected of them, but inevitably, the more polite of the two—or the less burdened—yielded. "What happened?" asked Saabir.

"We were discussing the proposal that Aliya received from Noor, and the ladies there were saying that Noor is Halai Memon, not Kutchi Memon, so she shouldn't accept it. I asked what was the big deal because we are all from the same damn place in India. They insisted there was a difference, but didn't know what to say when I asked them to explain. And then—"

"Well," said Saabir, "I've heard that the Halai Memons have felt excluded by the Kutchi Memons. You know, they're a very small community. They've now joined hands with the Surtis. For instance, they bury their dead in the same place as the Surtis in Riche Terre."

Shaheen sighed. "This is so complicated!" she said, "Sorry to be letting all this out on you two, but there is more that's upsetting me. I guess I am having a bad day. I really need to go back and see my Reiki healer and get rid of the negative energy... Apparently Sarah came across a website that said there's no difference between olive oil and Extra Virgin, and that both can be used at high temperatures. She accused me of spreading false information. I mean, to be fair, yes, recently I too read about that, but it was a genuine mistake on my part because I came across the information on a different website that seemed reliable. Sarah is out to get me. I think she's jealous of me and my happy marriage. We all know what Khalid does to her. I'm beginning to think she deserves it. Anyway, do you know that she was secretly in love with Parvez and was mad that he proposed to me? I won't be surprised if she's paid a visit to Choti Khala to cast some sort of curse on me. Thank God I don't believe in superstition."

Shaheen paused, sighed again, wiped Hannah's mouth, and looked across the room at her husband Zain talking to Khalid, Sarah's husband.

"I was planning to tell everyone about the benefits of brown rice, couscous and quinoa over white rice," she continued. "I got the information on a trustworthy website, but never mind. Let them all get diabetes! I just...don't like the negative energy Sarah exudes. Don't you feel it?"

Shaheen looked at Humeirah and Saabir; this time both returned silence and no more.

# VIII

## -Nirvana, or Reasons and their Unreason-

"I have been told that you attain nirvana when you learn to speak your own private language that is neither teachable nor translatable." Humeirah

Humeirah wondered about the silence in the house; the absence of footsteps that went up and down the staircase and resounded in the corridor outside her room. The scent of the strong, masculine deodorant that marked his movements was absent. She had also stopped hearing his loud boisterous tone on phone calls and was no longer startled by his sniffles and coughs. Not a sound. Nothing at all. And almost three weeks.

Both Shanthi and Warissah continued doing what they did every day and appeared indifferent to the change. Humeirah's anxiety grew exponentially. The feeling came as a surprise—and that was the problem. How could she miss *him,* of all persons?

Perhaps she had misinterpreted her feelings. Perhaps she was attached to him after all. What else? Her mind was at peace for a while, but the turbulence stirred her again. She became growingly obsessed with his absence, and the reason that had prompted it. Where was he? Why had he suddenly disappeared? She thought of asking Shanthi but feared being rebuffed once again.

"I don't really miss him," mumbled Humeirah to herself. "Maybe I am just curious and need to know where he is."

A convenient justification.

Finally, she gave in. "Where is Haider?"

Shanthi was chopping a few carrots and a cucumber.

"You don't know?" she said, without looking up.

Humeirah was silent. Shanthi sniggered and paused. "In South Africa on a business trip."

"When will he be back?"

Another pause.

"In a month's time."

After a few days, Humeirah felt restless again. "Yes," she reminded herself, "I was only *curious* about Haider's whereabouts. I couldn't possibly be missing him."

But it turned out to be one of the slowest months of her life. Although she now knew where he was and when he would be back, something didn't feel right. She dug into her heart and stumbled upon the same reason: *Maybe I just miss him.*

*But we don't spend time together, and he doesn't—*

*Then, why?*

*Maybe I suspect that he might be with Sana.*

She seemed pleased with this justification for a few days until she bumped into Sana in a mall in Phoenix. If Haider was with her, he would not have let come all the way there but sent the driver.

Then what was it? Humeirah's doubts set in again. "Maybe it's because he makes sure that Vijay looks after me. Maybe he cares after all."

But that was hardly the truth—Haider only sent Vijay to her after he had completed the tasks he had been assigned. Since there was always some time left before his official hours of duty were over, he would send him back to house so that he could be at the disposal of Shanthi, Warissah, and of course, Humeirah. He wanted to make sure that he got his money's worth out of employing him.

"Maybe I miss Haider because it's through his effort that this household can run. I certainly depend on him for my sustenance."

But the missing was directed at *him*, not at the ways in which he eased her life.

This exercise was not taking her anywhere. The reasons always felt right at first but ended up feeling inadequate.

Then, Humeirah stopped struggling with the emotions within.

Yes, she could not figure out why she missed him, but the truth was that she did.

A new feeling of peace, like a wave of calmness, swept over her.

*I don't have to justify everything.*

Humeirah reflected on the past and the times she had tried to make sense out of things. She remembered how she had justified her decision not to get close to Warissah; how she had justified liking tasteless food. Or the time when she had struggled to understand her father and how he had turned out to be. "I have always concocted reasons, connected chains and links so that everything could make sense. But everything makes sense only in the world of words where there are synonyms and antonyms for everything, and yet even these, we know, are not perfect."

Maybe, she thought, this was nirvana.

*I read that the only way I could reach a state of nirvana was to grow indifferent to the emotions around me, to turn into an ascetic. But how could I possibly do that: by suppressing my desire to be loved? By giving up on feeling hurt when Warissah turns her back on me? By denying that I miss Haider because reason dictates that I couldn't be missing someone who hurts me?*

*No. It is impossible to do that.*

She was silent—then had a realisation.

*Nirvana is not about not feeling... It's about not resisting feeling.*

*I don't know why I miss him, but I do, and maybe one day the reason will become clear to me.*

"It's just a habit you've grown used to and if you wait it out, it won't matter whether he's around," whispered the little voice, but Humeirah didn't hear it.

As Shanthi had predicted, Haider returned from the trip exactly one month later. Humeirah heard her open the front door, a pair of muffled voices exchanging conversation, and recognised the familiar shuffle of Haider's footsteps as he marched up the stairs and moved along the corridor towards his bedroom.

It made her smile a half smile. She would not speak to him or eat with him, but she would be comforted knowing he was around—and it didn't have to make sense.

# PART V

# Warissah

I

# -The Loud Voice in Humeirah's Head-

*"They* say: 'Don't look too deep, otherwise you'll get lost.'
I did and got lost. Not because there was too much—there was nothing." Humeirah

The loud voice in Humeirah's head: "You've done well, Humeirah."

Humeirah: "But the struggle that led to these realisations was unnecessary. I could have got here without going through pain; the pain was pointless. I could have been born in a family with people who would have allowed me to undergo more important struggles than this. This struggle in comparison seems so petty—"

The loud voice: "True. Many people reach this state without going through pain, but you are wrong about something: every society is the same. It's just that some people dwell in more atomised environments so that they're more isolated from one another to engage in gossip or manifest their shortcomings. Just be mindful that your realisations have pushed you to levels many would never reach—"

Humeirah: "If that's the case, I will move on. I will not let myself be overwhelmed by the knots in my life; I will find a way to turn them into sources of strength. Like *The Albatross*. With the consciousness that a weakness is but a strength, only couched differently."

The loud voice: "Yes, Humeirah. You are now ready."

Humeirah: "For what?"

The loud voice: "For the rest of the struggle. Your realisations only give you strength to move on and face other challenges."

Humeirah: "You mean I have to go through this again?"

The loud voice: "Not this, but other struggles."

Humeirah: "I wanted this to be the last big one. I thought I learned so much about people, about myself, and that I was finally armed to avoid more harm. So, what is the state of calmness and peace I'm experiencing at the moment?"

The loud voice: "You are in the eye of the cyclone. This is merely a comma in the sentence of life. For now, take deep breaths. The storm will rage again, the story will continue till its final full stop."

Humeirah: "What's the final full stop?"

The loud voice: "Death."

Humeirah: "So death will be a release from suffering?"

The loud voice: "Not released, because when you die you won't know it. You will never experience release from suffering."

Humeirah: "Oh."

The loud voice: "Don't despair, Humeirah. Life is about showing dignity and composure in both pain and happiness. Welcome happiness with open arms, and when in pain let it seep through you, but don't react disproportionately to either; remember that all emotions are transient. You don't want to look back on life and regret your actions."

# II

## -Life and Death-

"Sadly, you went looking for God above the sky and below the ground and because you didn't find him you thought he didn't exist.

Then you believed he was at the edge of the universe and when you still did not find him, you again believed he did not exist.

You didn't care to look hard enough. What you kept seeing above, below and at the edge were in truth the intestines of God. We are its microbes." The loud voice in Humeirah's head

*Freedom.*

Now it was clear.

In the evening, after putting away the book she was reading and drifting into a deep sleep, Humeirah found a new vehicle of expression: her dreams. It was akin to guiding a bridled horse in daytime and letting it go wild and free at night. The grace with which the horse gave expression to the newly found freedom revealed how well it had been trained.

For some time, Humeirah had a recurrent dream of an elderly lady dressed in white, who did not look like her mother, but whom she identified and spoke to as if she was. The lady would rest her hand on Humeirah's head, pull her towards her so that her head would rest against her chest, and say: "Don't worry, everything will be fine. You'll be fine." Humeirah would feel warm and reassured, and on opening her eyes, the feeling would linger.

Once awake, Humeirah would remember the lady as the one who had appeared in a dream just before she married Haider to tell her: "People like you shouldn't marry young."

What did the lady mean? Was she not fit for marriage? What was different about her compared to the others? Why did people say things and then walk away before explaining why? Elderly people, people who had experienced life longer than her, somehow did that, and it was upsetting.

After the dream, Humeirah mulled over the advice that had sowed doubt, but the wedding date had been set, and it would have been absurd to call it off—that too, because of a dream. Dreams didn't mean much to Gibran.

It was only later, after the knot was tied, that Humeirah understood that the lady had meant well and there was wisdom in what she had said. Now, in her dreams, while resting a hand on Humeirah's head, she sometimes said: "I warned you not to marry early. You had to get to know yourself before looking for someone who would compliment you. Some women don't need that. They are not haunted by the questions that haunt you."

Humeirah had thought about it for a long time. It wasn't as if the lady was suddenly articulate, volunteering an explanation after years of silence. Instead, it was her own realisation that she was now voicing to herself; her subconscious taking up the guise of the lady.

But the change in Humeirah's dreams didn't always involve the lady. Sometimes the thoughts she had during the day jumbled with ideas she had drawn from books, so that in her dreams, she would be figuring out answers to questions that haunted her. For instance, she now understood why many philosophers said that life was about pain and suffering, and sought to find ways to understand and accept it.

*Today, my unhappy marriage with Haider is the cause of my anguish; tomorrow, it will be something or someone else.*

*If Haider was not the cause of my anguish, it would probably be Warissah. I would seek to bridge the gap between us, and anything less would torment me.*

*I have neglected my own daughter so that I could divert my attention into figuring out how to fix my marriage.*

Humeirah would then feel guilty, followed by a different feeling.

*Sometimes the reason for our anguish is more material and concrete to some than others, depending on the nature of their own struggles.*

*Either way, we are all fighting monsters of some sort, and that is why life will always be about facing suffering; be it guilt, regret, loneliness, the desire for recognition...the desire for more.*

*The whole point is whether there's a way of holding on to the bigger picture of things as often as possible, and being aware of ourselves not as individuals, but as people caught up in the same predicament—and find solace therein.*

It also made sense to Humeirah to have felt like a misfit; to have been peculiar and to have asked strange questions.

But it was sad, she thought, to look back and remember the many times she had tried to have a meeting of minds with people around her; and was possibly still trying to, otherwise, she thought, why was she still here?

She had given much thought to her conversation with Saabir; what he had said about his own struggle; about hers; and how of all people she had ever known in life, she had felt a genuine connection with him.

*How can I blame Haider when he seems to be coping with the obstacles he has decided to overcome in life?*

*Do I have the right to qualify Shanthi as heartless when she is loving towards her own relatives, as well as my Warissah?*

*How can I harbour negative feelings for my dead father who lived a sheltered life and couldn't help being who he was?*

*Am I not myself enclosed in a small world and missing out on a better understanding of life and people?*

*And Sana. She too has latched onto the value system that suits her strengths and weaknesses; one she must have, consciously and subconsciously, tested through trial and error.*

*When we are stuck with people in the span of a few decades, it becomes easy for us to condemn them. And yet, each archetype has existed through the tides of time, and has lived, suffered, died, and still gone on to be born again, albeit not as the same being or soul.*

*There will always be a Tartuffe, a Don Quixote, a Bourgeois Gentilhomme, a Macbeth, a Blanche DuBois, and an Eva Perone in our lives. Similarly, there will always be a Shanthi, a Haider, an Ambareen, a Sana.*

*Who am I to be at war with their differences and condemn them when they deserve to be here, just as I?*

It did not mean that Humeirah had forgiven those who hurt her. No. To forgive and understand were completely different. She could not forgive them because it would make her a lesser human being. She was entitled to her emotions; to *feeling.*

*As animals we only had emotions at our disposal; but now that we have turned into human beings, we must cope with that big layer of reason that tries to take control of our emotions. This furtive tug-of-war between reason and emotions accounts for the turmoil and confusion in the decisions we take.*

*And all those questions that haunt us, all those puzzles about life, have already been broached in writings that are centuries old. What was of importance to our ancestors is still important to us today, and yet, how tempting to think that we are the first to wonder.*

So, what did Humeirah think of her role and purpose in the world in the bigger sphere of things?

She wanted to think of herself as different—even special, but knew better. She remembered Haider's erstwhile habit of extolling his virtues to her, expecting a look of admiration. The truth was that all of us wished to be unique and found rational ways to justify it to ourselves. But, ultimately, if morality differed so much in time and space, was there a reliable standard of right and wrong that made one more worthy than the other?

If so, what ultimate scale would it be based on? Material success? The probability of going to Heaven? These were all based on shaky foundations.

No. Humeirah realised that she was human too, and one day, she too would grow old and die like everyone else.

*How does it matter then that I have these thoughts, and that I can sometimes see through certain people and situations?*

Humeirah also mulled over how she felt tied down and imprisoned. She could divorce her husband, leave, and start life anew with someone who filled the void and made her happy. But these happily-ever-after stories sounded idealistic: if she broke the chains, she would only gain a limited measure of freedom. Maybe she would be free to do what she wanted, but she would still yearn for answers to the questions that haunted her. This search—the longing—the feeling of dissatisfaction—was the real culprit that kept her imprisoned.

Thereafter, Humeirah's interactions with Haider became scant. He didn't raise his hand to her because there was no reason for her to approach him, speak to him, and seek a connection. He also gave up his nightly intrusions. It almost seemed as if he had sensed a kind of godliness in her.

Humeirah started to go about life with calm indifference, and kept everyone at arm's length, accepting with grace what *They* offered, refraining from seeking any more than that. Every time she had to mingle with them, she waited to escape into the world she had moulded with her own hands.

III

# -Warissah's Prayer -

"Veni, Vidi, Vixi." Warissah

"'I came, I saw, I lived'?
But why?" Humeirah


From above, the volcanic crater of Trou aux Cerfs looked perfectly circular. It almost seemed as if on a visit to the island, a Brobdingnagian had left a giant doughnut behind, that, in time, had collected moss. That is what Trou aux Cerfs looked like—a giant doughnut.

Located at the centre of the island, itself elevated, and older than the rest of the land mass, the volcano overlooked houses that from a distance, appeared like tiny boxes with flattened roofs, when many were of various shapes and designs. These were in turn dotted with white specks that on closer look revealed themselves to be water tanks. Mountain-hills, distinct from one another—a thumbs-up sign on a mountain range; a steep and narrowing peak with a boulder perched atop; a row of three perky breasts, among others, and many named in French in emulation of their peculiarities—stood amid the vast expanse of light green, dark green, grey, blue and predominantly white. On a clear night long ago, Gibran had pointed at what he imagined to be a mass of land in the distance, lit, and told Warissah it was an island called Reunion.

The heart of the volcano's crater, Shanthi told her, was home to a huge monster that lay in deep slumber for millions of years. As it did, a long time ago, it was believed that it would wake up and spit up lava. Nobody knew when that would be. Nobody knew what was going on there. Nobody knew whether the refreshing, harmless-looking veil of dark green foliage that covered the interior and exterior of the crater disguised a terrible truth that Mauritians were not supposed to know. One only knew that the feet of the trees sunk into the crater's sides were nearer to the monster beneath, to its breathing and snoring. Maybe they, the trees, had the consciousness that in no time the monster would wake up, ravaging everything in its vicinity.

These unravelled mysteries gave the volcano an august air that ignited the imaginations of the old as the young. Warissah lived a few hundred metres away from Trou aux Cerfs, and mistook thunder for the volcanic monster's groans. On one occasion, when the thunder was very loud, she thought that the monster had woken up for good.

Questions kept haunting her: would the monster finally wake up and vomit volumes of that thick orange phlegm called lava? She had watched a movie where people were trying to escape from it, and those who fell into it, either died or disappeared. Would the lava also swallow her until there was nothing left? And what about the early-morning joggers who circled the crater? Where would they run to if the volcano erupted? And why was it called *Trou aux Cerfs*—the hole (or shelter) of deer? Where were the deer? Sometimes she believed she had caught glimpses of their antlers, but they ended up being wild overgrown branches.

If the monster did wake up, Warissah told herself she would hide in the playroom and lock the door. She was certain that the lava would only be able to come up to the door and walls, perhaps eat away the exposed layers, but leave her untouched.

Still, what would happen to everyone else? Mummy would be upstairs—the lava couldn't reach there; Ee-jay would be in the car and could drive away to his house; Ti would be alone in the kitchen—maybe she could come and hide with her in the playroom.

***

It was one of those afternoons when Warissah was waiting for Ustaad Ashraf to come home for the lessons. Earlier, she had handed over Dolly to Shanthi for safekeeping—something she never failed to do before Ustaad Ashraf appeared at the front door.

Shanthi had had to find a way around Warissah's habit of hiding Dolly behind the fridge, since the doll was getting dirtier by the day.

"We will have to throw Dolly into the dustbin if you keep doing that."

Warissah had imagined Dolly lying on top of a stinky pile of broken eggshells, empty milk cartons and the leftovers of grated carrots and cucumbers; the Dustbin Man arriving in his big dark green lorry, as he did every so often, carrying everything away, including Dolly, and dump it all in a wide expanse of land in Mont Roches that Ee-jay had pointed out, where everything was set on fire, and where the grass across it and the mountain-hill right behind looked charred and gloomy.

"What will happen if the volcano explodes and the orange from it touches me?" asked Warissah, as Ustaad Ashraf settled down at the table to begin the lesson.

"What are you talking about?" he said, impatient to start the class. Habituated to unusual and unrelated questions from the children he taught, Warissah's questions were more unusual and unrelated.

"If the volcano explodes, will the orange lava kill me?"

"No, it won't... But let's talk about this later. First things first: let's start with the alphabet." Warissah opened her qaida half-heartedly and recited the Arabic alphabets to perfection. She couldn't wait to ask the question again, but soon after, it was time for stories about Prophet Muhammad. Warissah shut her qaida and was about to speak.

"You shouldn't close your qaida so roughly—it's disrespectful," said Ustaad Ashraf, taking the book, opening it and making a display of how to close it.

Then he placed the qaida before her and opened it again. "Now, do it."

With care and attention, Warissah closed it gently.

"Good. Now tell me what you wanted to know."

"Will the volcano explode?"

"Allah will decide that."

"But if Allah decides to do that, will I die?"

"That's in Allah's hands too. If Allah wishes for you to die, you will die. If Allah wishes for you to stay alive, you will live."

"What will happen when I die?"

"You will go to Heaven or Hell depending on whether you were a good girl or a naughty one."

The mention of Heaven and Hell sounded familiar. "You mean, just like Nana?"

"Yes, just like Nana."

"What happens in Heaven and Hell?"

"In Heaven there are pure white angels who will be nice to you and give you sweets and chocolates, and you will live in a castle and have lots of maids to take care of you. In Hell, there will be a big cauldron of boiling water with scary shaitans dancing around, and if you are naughty, you will be pushed into it."

Warissah's eyes grew wide; but she remained quiet. "Where did Nana go? I want to go where he went."

"I don't know, Warissah. If your Nana was a good man, he would go to Heaven and if he was a bad man he would go to Hell."

"But my Nana was not bad. My Nana will go to Heaven."

"Allah will decide that. It's simple, Warissah. To be a good person and to go to Heaven, you must pray five times a day and love Allah. If your Nana did that, he will go to Heaven, Insha Allah."

"But my Nana did not pray five times. He prayed once only, in the morning only. And sometimes in the afternoon."

Ustaad Ashraf shifted in his chair, and before she could ask further questions, he said: "Do you pray, Warissah?"

Warissah shook her head hesitantly, then guiltily, on the verge of tears. Ustaad Ashraf would get angry now.

"Warissah, you must be a good girl. The children who come to the masjid pray five times. Didn't I teach you how to pray?"

The lecture went on. Warissah had stopped paying attention, tormented with thoughts of her Nana who had been shoved into a big cauldron of boiling water.

***

"Nonsense!" Shanthi said, after Warissah recounted what Ustaad Ashraf had told her. "I don't know what these people are teaching you. I have friends who are Muslims and aren't taught such ridiculous things. Your Nana will certainly go to Heaven. In fact, he is in Heaven *now*, and one day, when you grow old and die, you will see him again."

That evening, as Warissah climbed into bed and Dolly was tucked in next to her, she waited for Shanthi to turn off the light and close the door. Then, she sat up, drew the palms of her hands together and whispered: "Please, Allah, don't let my Nana burn in boiling water. He doesn't like it when it's hot. He will get hurt. Please, Allah, let my Nana go to Heaven. Please, Allah, he will be happy there because he needs someone to take care of him and he also likes chocolates. Please, Allah, I promise I will be a good girl. I will stop playing with Dolly and I will pray five times. Please, Allah."

Finally, Warissah drew the covers over her, and heavy-heartedly, pushed Dolly to the edge of the bed till she rolled over and dropped onto the floor.

That night, Warissah dreamt of her Nana who emerged through the volcano and asked her to pack her bags because they had to flee a horde of shaitans chasing him.

IV

# -That Fateful Day-

"Most knowledge lacks absoluteness to be an undeniable truth." Humeirah

Warissah tugged at the sleeve of Ambareen's salwar kameez. It was a Sunday afternoon and she wanted to go to Balfour Garden. Not long ago, she had divided her weekends between her grandfather and her aunt, but that had changed. Now she only spent them with the latter.

Everyone was worried that Warissah would notice the change, so they tried to disguise it by entertaining the most trivial requests. Lately, as a result, she had grown more persistent in her demands.

On the way to the park, she interrupted the silence: "An-ny-Breen, you know, my friend Sangreem has a big white house near Balfour."

"Who is Sangreem?" Ambareen knew most of the students in the kindergarten.

"Sangreem is Miss Rose's favourite."

"She means *Sandrine*," said an amused Vijay. "It's the girl I once dropped off from school since her mother was busy."

"Ah, yes," said Ambareen, and then turned to Warissah. "Why do you say that my jaan? Miss Rose likes you too."

"No, she is nice only to Sangreem. She never gets angry with her."

"I'm sure Miss Rose loves you too; she just doesn't show it. It's impossible for grown-ups to hate children."

Warissah tried to make sense of what her aunt had said. She had to be right.

Vijay dropped Ambareen and Warissah at the entrance of Balfour Garden, parked outside, in a lane hugged by interwoven houses, a tabajie, a makeshift synagogue; too narrow to accommodate the clamour of vehicles and the pent-up frustration of their drivers. He reclined his seat and settled in to take a nap.

At the park, Warissah wished to go through the ritual she had established, of first seeing the waterfall in the gorges. She and Ambareen walked up to it, stood by the fence, and looked towards the northeastern end. "I want to see the white castle!" Warissah said. Ambareen lifted Warissah to get a quick glimpse of the structure next to the waterfall. Then she pointed to the pen of tortoises and walked to it hand-in-hand with her aunt. There were six, all still, some in puddles of muddy water, others withdrawn in their shells, and across the pen, was "GIANT ALDABRA TORTOISE PEN ".

"Warissah, these tortoises you see were born before you and will die after you."

"After I am old?"

Ambareen nodded.

"An-ny-Breen, were they born before you?"

"Yes."

"Were they here when Nana was little?"

"Yes."

Warissah continued to look at them.

"An-ny-Breen, Miss Monique said there's a tortoise and a hare, and the hare is always fast, but the tortoise is slow and that's why the tortoise wins the race. I am also slow like the tortoise, An-ny-Breen, but I don't win any races."

Ambareen smiled. "Don't worry, Warissah. You will win all the races soon."

Warissah then pointed at the monkey bars on the children's playground, and while walking towards it, they crossed a narrow canal of moving water, loud and voluminous, so that she clasped her aunt's hand more tightly.

Ee-jay had said it was dangerous, and if one fell into it, one could be carried all the way from Rose Hill to Beau Bassin by strong currents, drown, and even die.

Before climbing the monkey bars, Warissah cried out: "An-ny-Breen, play with me!"

"No, my jaan. I can't. I'm too big for this."

Ambareen sat down on one of the concrete benches where she could keep an eye on her niece. Warissah struggled with the swing, both a bit high and impossible to keep still enough to climb. Ambareen walked to her.

Once Warissah was carefully seated, she cried out: "Push me...Push me, An-ny-Breen."

"Why don't you leave your doll with me so that you can sit properly?"

Warissah clung to Dolly's arm as well as the chain of the swing, shaking her head.

When Ambareen turned around to walk away, Warissah piped in again: "An-ny-Breen, look at me. I'm a bird."

Ambareen smiled, recognising the subterfuge.

"All right. I'll be here for a bit."

Ambareen wanted to give Kareem a call. There was a lot of planning to do for their upcoming wedding, she reasoned—in truth it was merely an excuse. More than anything, she wanted to connect with him, more so since his mother Fatima had prohibited it. She didn't let him speak to her on the phone, let alone meet. "Ena mofin ladan," is what she had said, adding that it could curse their union since, in the time of the Prophet—whose life, she said, we were under the obligation to emulate—those who were engaged or betrothed did not communicate with each other till *after* the nikah ceremony.

"Yes, but there were no phones at that time," Kareem had said.

"Stop arguing! I am your mother. I know what's good for you. You know what they say: that even if you carry your mother on your shoulders and perform tawaf around the Kaabah, you won't be able to pay her back for the birth pangs she went through for you."

Warissah hopped from the swing, went to the merry-go-round, sat down and shouted: "Move me, move me, An-ny-Breen."

"It's not safe for you to be on the merry-go-round by yourself. There must be other children on it for you to play."

"Where are they?"

"They will come later, jaan. All right, go and sit on it for a while and I'll push you around gently. But hold on tight to the handles."

Later, satiated with dizziness, Warissah urged her aunt to stop the merry-go-round, jumped off and sprang towards the swing. Ambareen followed her.

"Don't swing me, An-ny-Breen. I can swing on my own."

"OK, but you won't be able to swing by yourself if you hold your doll. I'll keep it for you."

But Warissah was adamant. Once she seemed settled and confident, Ambareen walked to the bench and called Kareem.

The swing picked up momentum so that the rush of air on Warissah's face was exhilarating, the back-and-forth making her stomach churn. Whenever the swing ascended to a peak, fear mixed with delight, and as she became used to the feeling, every time she drew closer to the patchy network of leaves from surrounding trees, she noticed how sunlight filled the interstices and created bold patterns.

But Warissah struggled to hold the doll and the chain of the swing at the same time, and gradually lost power over her grip so that it fluttered out of her hand and landed further away. Warissah waited for the swing to slow down, then jumped and walked over to it. But while leaning over to pick it up, she slipped over a wet patch of mud and fell into a pit.

Ambareen witnessed it. She dropped everything and ran towards her, shouting, hoping someone would help. The security guard's house stood on the side of the park, but no one was in sight.

Ambareen broke into sobs, calling for help, and ran outside the garden on limbs that felt wobbly. She tapped on the car window and Vijay woke up.

Eight feet deep, the pit had been dug out the day before while erecting a monument. Work had only just started. Nobody had envisaged that a child would wander to this corner of the garden.

In the pit, Vijay saw Warissah's limp body in a puddle of muddy water, amid concrete slabs, rocks, empty cartons of juice, crumpled up wastepaper and depressed plastic bottles. Without hesitating, he jumped in, picked her up, and hauled himself up with the support of debris that jutted out from its sides.

There was a gaping wound on the left side of her small head and blood oozed out in volumes unbelievably disproportionate to the size of the opening.

Ambareen and Vijay touched Warissah's cheek, her forehead, shook her gently then forcefully, and called out her name in panic and despair. Warissah's body only moved in rhythm to the jolts.

"We have to take her to the hospital," said Vijay, making his way towards the park's exit. Ambareen, out of her wits, followed him, and both laid Warissah in the rear of the car.

"Which hospital?" she asked.

"Clinique Mauricienne is the nearest, but there must be traffic right now."

"Let's go to Clinique Darné. It's closer to the house and we know all the doctors there. I'll call Haider."

Throughout the journey to Floreal, despite Vijay and Ambareen's ministrations, Warissah remained unconscious.

***

A few metres from the children's playground, Dolly lay in the grass, shabby and ragged as ever, drowned in mud.

While Warissah fought for her life in hospital, the doll stayed in the open, exposed to the rain.

The next morning, a man by the name of Raj, an independent contractor hired to set the monument's foundation, chanced upon it and decided to take it to his house. There, he wiped it, washed and dried its dress and put it back on the following morning before handing it to his two daughters who had never before owned one.

The younger one wouldn't part with it; the other couldn't get over the tinkle of the metal bead and when no one was looking, drew a hammer out from her father's toolbox and broke it open.

V

# -The Artist's Favourite Crayon-

"Sadly, it's only when you say, 'You are!' that I am." Humeirah

Shanthi knocked on Humeirah's bedroom door in a language that conveyed urgency. An ominous portent. She didn't wait but barged in and headed towards Humeirah who was in bed, lost in thought.

Barely two months had elapsed since Gibran's demise.

"Warissah has been in an accident. She's been admitted to casualty in Darné."

Humeirah's expression changed. Both rushed out of the room.

Haider was in the driveway, about to open the car door.

"What happened?" asked Humeirah.

"I don't know. I just got the news."

Haider, Humeirah and Shanthi climbed into the car, for once harbouring the same emotion, and headed towards the hospital not far away.

Warissah was in the casualty ward of Clinique Darné, and word was going around that she had lapsed into a coma. Other members of the family had gathered and looked anxious—or put on solemn appearances.

Haider went up to them while Humeirah found out where her daughter was, and walked up to the room, Shanthi following her.

Finally, Humeirah and Shanthi looked at Warissah through a glass separating them. Warissah's frail body lay in bed, plugged into tubes that led to a battery of machines.

"What's happened to our baby?" cried Shanthi. "What's happened to Baby Warissah? Our angel..."

Humeirah wished she could reach out and hold her daughter. Was she unconscious—or dead and inexistent?

Not far away, Ambareen sat on a bench, hugging the shoulder of another relative, sobbing. Humeirah noticed her shalwar khameez that now looked like a butcher's apron. It was Warissah's blood—*her daughter's* blood.

Humeirah moved closer to her sister-in-law who looked up through a pair of bloodshot eyes. "It wasn't my fault! I promise!" she said and recounted what had happened in Balfour.

Humeirah touched her shoulder gently. "It wasn't your fault."

Ambareen lowered her head and continued to cry, while Humeirah moved to a corner of the corridor and stood in the hall with her back against the wall. Relatives and friends uttered words of comfort:

"Don't worry, everything will be all right".

"Be patient".

"Pray for her".

Humeirah returned to her pensive state. She hadn't shed a tear since hearing the news—there were already whispers.

"It was the same when her father died, remember?" Fatima whispered to another.

Ambareen's emotional outburst appeared more normal.

"After all, it was an *accident*. It could have happened to *any* child," *They* whispered.

The blame, it was implied, was entirely Humeirah's since it was due to *her* neglect that Ambareen had had to take care of the child.

"Of course," *They* adde*d*, "Ambareen can't be expected to take on the responsibilities of a mother. You must evaluate the root cause of everything."

A man of noticeable stature, in a green gown, with pepper-and-salt hair and a calm appearance, stepped out of one of the rooms in the casualty ward. Dr. Pillay asked to see Warissah's parents, but Haider had stepped out to answer a phone call and Humeirah to get water. Ambareen noticed him surveying the hall.

"Doctor, I am Warissah's aunt. I don't know where her parents are right now. What happened to her, Doctor? Warissah is very close to me. What happened—?"

"Her condition is stable, but the injuries are quite deep. Nothing can be said for now. She is very young, so this could play out in favour of surgery but also against. Let's hope for the best and wait; then we'll think of how to proceed."

Ambareen continued to look at the doctor. "But she will be fine, won't she? She is young. Nothing can happen to her."

"Don't worry, we are trying our best. Let's pray for her recovery."

In the early days, Dr. Pillay would freeze in the face of comforting people in similar scenarios, fumbling in his sentences and displaying awkward gestures. Eventually he turned to his seniors, observing and imitating them, and somehow grew better at the task. But over the years, he had started to put in less and less effort, immune to the effusion of emotions and the melodrama that often ensued.

Because his reaction stopped matching the severity of the situation, he came up with an excuse to justify it, telling his patients or their relatives: "I'm sorry, I understand what you're going through and it's terrible, but I can't afford to get upset, otherwise I myself will have a heart attack. That's why I try to stay calm and indifferent."

Through experience, Dr. Pillay had also learned to tailor responses in proportion to the knowledge and understanding of people he interacted with since he quickly realised that everyone received information differently.

Now, he recognised the case to be one where the family would face a tragedy. There were multiple injuries, internal bleeding, and the patient was very young. He knew that his predictions in this one would be on point. If the patient did come out of the coma, she would suffer physical and mental impairment for the rest of her life.

But how could he tell Warissah's relatives the truth? The lady he had met earlier had given him an idea where to set the baseline. Maybe, he thought, the patient's parents would be different, and he could be more honest with them about the prognosis.

Then again, who could tell? A patient could still come out of a similar situation, cured and rehabilitated. There were always exceptions—or *miracles*, so that even the aunt, despite the outbursts and platitudes, could end up being right.

Humeirah and Haider reappeared in the hall at the same time. Ambareen rushed towards them.

"Dr. Pillay just said...Warissah won't make it. Oh God...Warissah won't make it," she said, amid sobs.

Humeirah stood still, Haider's expression grew graver. "What did he say exactly?" he asked.

"Dr. Pillay said that if she undergoes surgery now, she will die."

"Is that all he said?"

"Yes... yes..."

Haider looked away. Humeirah crossed her arms and stared at the ground.

Clearly, Ambareen had misconstrued Dr. Pillay's message, but maybe she had transmitted what she had not heard but sensed, for as animals gifted with instinct, we overlooked or downplayed our ability to discern truth disguised by deceit or decorum. It was our faith in reason, rationalism and the text that let us down.

Haider, Humeirah, and Ambareen stood in a cluster in silence.

Then, Ambareen resumed: "No. She won't die. Nobody dies this young. She was perfectly all right yesterday. Remember? I bought her a new dress for Dolly."

"Warissah will get well, Ambareen," said Haider. "Don't you worry. I know Dr. Pillay very well. I've done him many favours in the past. He will find a way. And then, God will help us. He always helps those who are good, and we are good people."

Humeirah looked at them in turn. Had she told them about the next book she wished to buy, they would have reacted indignantly and said: "This is *not* the time for it, Humeirah." And yet—

But the world, she thought—at least this one—was governed by a different constant; one accepted and embraced by the numbers, and in it, she was only a minority.

Thoughts, including Humeirah's, were fortunately inaudible, so Ambareen went on: "You know, last week, Warissah got on top of the table and was playing with something there. She was about to fall but I caught her on time: maybe that was a sign from God, maybe God was trying to tell me that Warissah won't live long. Oh! Why wasn't I wary of the sign? Why didn't I spend more time with her?"

Ambareen broke into louder sobs. Humeirah felt claustrophobic. She walked up to the room in the casualty ward and peered through the glass, watching her daughter's chest rise and fall. The rule, she thought, was to live and breathe; death was the inevitable event that changed the course of things through circumventing illness or accident.

Why should she then be surprised?

Humeirah held back all afternoon, indulging in further exercises of rationalising the tragedy. Finally, in the evening, when no one was around, her eyes welled up.

*This didn't happen because of a disease, but an...event; an accident. It could have been prevented. It would have merely taken a slight modification in my routine—in what happened that day.*

*If Papa was still alive, if I had been there, if it had just rained...*

Humeirah realised how everything about life hinged on a set of givens; the fiction of constancy and predictability, when in truth everything was capricious and vulnerable. At the thought of losing Warissah, an allegory was conjured up in her mind.

Humeirah imagined feeling like an artist deprived of one of her favourite crayons, and whose future works from then on would be less colourful than they could have been.

Yes.

She couldn't find the words to express her pain, and her thoughts were still muddled from the shock, but this made sense and soothed her as much as it could.

What she didn't realise then, was that life was in a constant flux and the artist would learn to make do without the crayon—in fact she would get hold of other colours to add to the beauty of what she wanted to depict. And one day, the memory of her loss would start fading, and as time would go by, she would realise that she had learned to cope despite everything—despite the brokenness.

VI

## -Those Who Seem to Know-

"Explaining is another word for justifying." Humeirah

It had been a hellish week for Humeirah, Haider, Ambareen and Shanthi who had taken turns to keep an eye on Warissah at Clinique Darné. Mr. and Mrs. Shah had phoned, promising to fly down from the UK at the soonest. Relatives, friends, and friends of friends, more curious than concerned, crowded the hospital. They asked the same questions and received the same replies:
"How is she?"
"Not very good."
"What did the doctor say?"
"We have to wait."
"How many days now?"
"Four"
...
"Five"
...
"Ten"
...
"Twelve"

Many of those on visit, young and old, wondered how it would feel if they too were faced with similar circumstances.

Haider was agitated. He phoned the Municipality and blamed them for their negligence. How could they have left such a deep pit unfilled and uncovered when a children's playground was nearby? Threatening to hire the best lawyer in town to sue the authorities, he added that if they didn't cover the pit in the next two days, he would make sure that whoever was involved would lose his or her job and never find work. Those in his company conceded, and after he hung up, listed their connections in the legal profession, reassuring him that he should not hesitate if he needed help.

Sometimes, in gatherings at his house, they fired up his temper by commenting on other acts of negligence by the authorities: a burst pipe that made road users in the area vulnerable; an electric pole that now leaned to the side, Tower-of-Pisa style, following the last wind gusts of a cyclone, posing a risk to travellers and passersby. It was The System that was inefficient and corrupt, they added, and it was high time someone did something; a rhetoric that had been repeated ad nauseam in this venue as well as comparable ones.

In the meantime, Dr. Pillay came around almost every day to monitor the progress of the patient. "Give it time," he said.

One week went by: "Give it time."

Then, ten days.

Two weeks later, Dr. Pillay walked out of the operation theatre after performing a second round of surgery on Warissah.

The first had gone rather well, but more had to be done, he had then said. This time however, as he came up to Haider and Humeirah, he shook his head: "We'll have to disconnect the machines." He didn't have time to explain—an uproar ensued.

Zain, and then Shaheen, embraced Haider as the latter burst into loud sobs. Shanthi was comforted by her daughter-in-law Deepa; Vijay by Anjili; Ambareen by Mr. and Mrs. Shah. A silent and withdrawn Humeirah walked away, far from the crowd.

But everyone understood, everyone cooperated, everyone drove the members of the family home in preparation of the rituals following the tragedy.

***

While the funeral arrangements were being made by those-who-seemed-to-know, Humeirah sat in a corner of the sitting room of her house, staring into her lap. The chairs and sofas had been pushed against the wall, and a carpet laid to accommodate the numbers. If Humeirah had had her way, she would have stayed in the bedroom.

"She is feeling guilty," *They* whispered. "See. She wasn't a good mother and is regretting it."

"Cruel and heartless," said another.

People adopted sitting or standing positions wherever they could, scanning the room for members of the family of the deceased, observing every movement, interpreting thoughts and statements every time lips were twitched and tears were dropped.

As part of the funeral rites, the mirrors in the house had been covered with towels and sheets.

"What's this for?" Humeirah had asked.

"This is the way it's done. This is tradition," replied a man who-seemed-to-know.

"What's this for?" Humeirah had asked another who-seemed-to-know.

"These mirrors are hidden to prevent people from seeing something from the other world. When someone dies, souls from the other world visit the house of the deceased. If we look into mirrors, we will see them and get scared. And they too will get annoyed."

"What's this for?" Humeirah had asked a woman who-seemed-to-know.

"Women have very fertile imaginations. We don't want them to look into mirrors when someone has died, because they will claim to have seen something from the other world." With a solemn and knowing smile, she added: "Women are always imagining things."

Humeirah observed everyone perform rituals with care and attention. Ladies who were usually relegated to the status of insignificant housewives became the most important people because they seemed to know.

They seemed to know the practices and superstitions that accompanied the funeral process, and this gave them the authority to shout out orders to everyone. This was their special moment, and as maestros, they exploited the privilege and position of power.

A basket of red roses was brought in, and one by one, each stalk was appended to white strings of cloth by ladies who had gathered around one of the maestros who-seemed-to-know who detailed the process.

What was meant to be an attempt to add colour to the pallid mood and atmosphere took up the ethos of a religious ritual, so that the difference between performing a compulsory religious ritual and merely decorating was blurred.

Humeirah could feel her head throbbing and wished she could ask the little voice in her head to be quiet. Maybe she shouldn't have asked questions to those-who-seemed-to-know. She wished she could spend a few moments looking at her daughter without the presence of people as well as their traditions, totems, superstitions and unnecessary complications. Somebody had died—*her daughter*—had died. She wanted to feel it, accept it, come to terms with it—and do it alone.

Warissah's limp body was laid on the carpeted ground after being wiped and wrapped in seamless pieces of white cotton cloth, covered from head to toe. The strings of red roses had been placed across the thick white bundle in horizontal lines. Many noticed the particularity of this funeral—a *short* bundle compared to the ones they were used to.

Out of nowhere, a voice weak with crying, said: "I want to see Warissah's face one last time."

It was Ambareen.

"How can you do that?" said one who-seemed-to-know. "You can't see her face. It's a sin."

"Why is it a sin?" retorted another, who also seemed-to-know. "There's nothing wrong with that. God never forbade that. Let her do what she wants. It's her niece."

A pseudo-academic discussion ensued.

"It's OK to look at the face *before* the ritual of ghusl, not after," said another.

The crowd paid close attention, taking in as much as possible, brewing a story to be recounted later. The discussion ended. A few egos were inflated; many others, bruised. The conclusion was that Ambareen could see Warissah's face, but by then Ambareen had lost the spontaneity. Perfunctorily, she approached the body, uncovered the hood, stole a self-conscious glance, readjusted the hood, and moved away. Nothing had changed: her grief had not been slightly assuaged.

Warissah's body was carried out of the house by Haider. A cluster of men chanting Arabic verses accompanied him to the funeral van outside. Humeirah followed their movements. She would never see her daughter again—this was the real end.

After the men had stepped outside, and the room felt bare, the others turned around to observe her, some discreetly, others not. At the very least, they expected her to cry. This time, she did; but quietly.

***

Later that evening, after everyone had left, Humeirah, who hadn't moved from the corner of the sitting room, felt overwhelmed by a feeling of purposelessness.

What was the value of Warissah's life? she wondered. Someone else, at this exact point, maybe in a different part of the world, was undergoing the same pain after losing a child.

Did she, the mother, also question the meaning of life? The purpose of all this?

Did she also feel that her world was about to crumble? That nobody understood her?

Humeirah's thoughts went to her father's cousin who had lost a teenage daughter in a car accident; her late mother's relative in India whose five-year-old had been mauled by a tiger at a reserve; a cousin in London whose daughter had dropped from a balcony onto a parked moped and sustained fatal brain injuries. Humeirah now had an inkling of what they had endured.

Surely, they too had then been lonely, thinking they were the only ones to feel that way, and yet, Humeirah realised, in the bigger sphere of things, these deaths meant nothing. From above, these deaths were merely flickers of light that had been extinguished in random locations on the Earth's surface—and replaced with new ones with the birth of new individuals. There were after all so many of us.

Was mourning her daughter's death therefore ridiculous?

*No.*

While this was what she would have observed from above, in the manner of an omniscient entity, detached and supposedly objective, Humeirah told herself she was *not* above—she was down here at the same level as everyone, and it meant that she was *Warissah's mother* and nobody else's. Nobody else had known and experienced Warissah the way she had.

Who was Warissah in the greater scheme of things? Nobody. Who was Humeirah? Again, nobody. But the relationship had existed, and while it did, Warissah had mattered.

Humeirah reached a conclusion that day—she had no reason to stay back. Once upon a time, a cord had tied her to her world; one that had given her a reason to fight and survive, but more importantly, to stay back. That cord—an umbilical cord—had been Warissah.

Now, nothing tied her down; nothing held her back. She was free to leave, free to be autonomous.

VII

# -Humeirah, The Artist-

"Your children shield you from your past…if you let them." Humeirah

The house had grown quiet. Not that it had been very lively, but there had been a bustle with Shanthi preparing meals in the kitchen and pottering around in the house and garden; Vijay coming in and out to drop something off or pick someone up; trays of food going up the stairs to Humeirah's bedroom and returning empty—and then Warissah had been there, not far, usually in the playroom with Dolly and her toys.

In the evening, when everything would slow down and come to a halt, Haider would walk into the house, introducing an air of busyness and purpose. Shanthi would rush to make tea, and by the time she would serve it to him, he would be in front of the TV, toying with the remote control, changing channels. After some time, he would disappear into his room and Shanthi would clean up and then retire. The members of the household had grown used to the rut of this routine, but now that it had suffered a tremor, they had grown conscious of its loss.

Haider stopped meeting with his friends after work and returned home earlier than usual. He was glum within, and the glumness revealed itself without restraint. He spent most of his time reciting the Quran on the advice of Ustaad Ashraf, and since he was in the house more often, Shanthi prepared dinner every day so that Humeirah had fresh supplies of food—not that it mattered. She barely ate, or often, the meal remained untouched.

In the subdued silence that loomed in the house, Shanthi's disdain for Humeirah had disappeared—or been put on hold. Instead, she diverted her attention to Anusha and Valesha, more protective than ever, and saw danger in everything, so that it got in their way of loving her.

Shanthi also barely exchanged a word with Vijay who had retreated into himself, and all she did was sigh and mutter over and over to him and whoever she came across: "Never mind, God willed it. My Warissah is with her Nana and Nani. They will keep an eye on her."

***

Humeirah was about to enter the kitchen to get a glass of water when there was a knock on the door. She thought of attending to it—she too had loosened up and in a spirit of cooperation, did what she could to avoid treading on anyone's toes, taking on some of the chores that were usually Shanthi's.

"Hello," said the person as she opened the door. "My sincere condolences. I never seem to be around when I should. I'm terribly sorry for your loss."

Humeirah's face lit up and her eyes welled up.

"Please come in, Saabir. Have a seat."

Both walked to the sitting room.

Saabir was about to speak, but Humeirah noticed and didn't wait.

"I've lost so much in a few days, Saabir. Yes, I wasn't close to my daughter, but she was what I had closest to me. She knew when I was in pain and was there for me. What she must have gone through! I can't help being haunted by thoughts of how young she is—*was*. And the image of her lying in that bed in hospital... I couldn't speak to her, Saabir. I couldn't reach out to her and tell her I was there. My baby."

Humeirah put her hand on her mouth to muffle the sobs. New thoughts plagued her ever since her daughter had passed away. This time she knew she wouldn't recover so easily.

Saabir was about to say something, but she continued: "Tell me, Saabir, these writers we read don't have anyone to share their thoughts with, right? When they express themselves, they gain validation. It almost feels as if they want to reach out to someone who thinks like them; someone who feels the same way they do."

Saabir peered at Humeirah, who, soon after, stared at the ground. He could tell that she had been starved for someone who would listen to her.

"Maybe we should talk about something else," she finally said. "What have you been reading?"

"Right now, I'm rereading Ralph Waldo Emerson's. I read it in my early twenties, but I've forgotten most of it."

"I understand. I often feel inadequate because I don't remember most of what I have read. All I can hope for is that the most pivotal ideas would permeate my subconscious and become permanent thought-shifters."

"That makes two of us, Humeirah. Often, all that's left of a book in its afterlife is a mood, an emotion, or an anecdote or two."

Humeirah paused to reflect on that, then nodded.

"Let me serve you something to drink. Would you like something hot or cold?"

Humeirah headed towards the kitchen where Shanthi was doing the dishes.

"So, let me guess: you are enjoying yourself. How easy it is for you to get over things, sit and entertain people."

Humeirah stopped and stared at her.

"You don't feel what we feel," Shanthi went on, "You don't suffer as we do. I was the one who brought her up, not you."

Humeirah felt too tired to put up a protest. She remembered a thought that had marked her: that pain was unquantifiable, so that saying that someone suffered more than another was only a partial assessment. A man who lived by himself on a hill could be suffering more than a woman who witnessed the death of her child in a brutal accident.

Humeirah walked over to the cabinet, drew out two mugs and followed up with other steps to brew coffee. She heard Shanthi's sniffles and out of the corner of her eye, noticed her wiping her face with her wrists.

Shanthi was in pain too, thought Humeirah, and blaming and attacking her as she had done was a means to negotiate with it. She returned to the sitting room, handed one of the mugs to Saabir and sat down.

"I noticed that all the mirrors in the house are covered."

"Yes," said Humeirah, "a common tradition after someone has died, apparently to prevent us from seeing things, since we have fertile imaginations. But I'm not sure. Everyone has different reasons for the same practices."

"I understand that. Coming up with reasons and justifications is never hard. Just a matter of being clever and clever sounding. You've probably realised how we keep changing our minds about why things are the way they are. In fact, there seem  to  be more reasons than people to explain things."

"Oh Saabir, yes. That has always perturbed me. Doesn't it reveal how fickle minded we are, and therefore, how truth is not dependable?

"On the contrary, I believe we're all unnecessarily fixated with the notion of constancy, as if the more constant we are about a thought or idea, the more dependable and sound it is. Instead, we should be happy that the truth is always changing. It shows we are still thinking. If we stopped and were satisfied with what we had, truth would turn into dogma."

"I never really saw it in that way."

Both continued to sip their coffee.

"I want to know, Saabir. Wanting to communicate desperately with outsiders; searching for others who suffer and understand what is going on—is this weakness? Is such profound dependence on people a weakness?"

"Why should it? It's a human need and it has to be embraced. Why should we suppress our humanness? Remember, even the greatest artists and thinkers—Van Gogh and Nietzsche, for example—suffered tremendous anguish during their lifetime because they were not recognised and validated for what they felt; for what they knew, for what they could foresee. For instance, Van Gogh committed suicide at thirty-seven and died poor. Nietzsche lost his mind in his forties. Both were misunderstood geniuses and lived on the fringes of society—although I remember Nietzsche's advice that while we should enjoy solitude, people are important too. They should be like gardens in our lives, or the music over the waters at the end of the evening. He went on to say that we have to make sure that the solitude we dwell in is a *good* one, meaning that we aren't living as active contrarians, since it would take away the breadth and objectivity with which we would wish to continue viewing the world."

"Yes, Saabir, as much as I yearn to be on my own, I realise the importance of having people around, and how necessary it is to one's well-being."

"We must be careful about how we manage our feelings and emotions. It's easy to get carried away and believe in some sort of uniqueness and superiority, and so many fall in the trap. But who defines worth? No one. After all, we still must suffer the same stages of life as everyone. What I'm saying is that the innate ability to feel deeply could be put to good use—it doesn't have to be a weakness—provided you create something out of it. Remember, you see things others don't. Your task, Humeirah, is to translate what you see for other people who are seeking it and devise a language to express it. Your task is to show them how in between the green and blue, there are other shades."

Humeirah nodded. "Yes, the so-called sane ones see the green and the blue. The artist, the so-called lunatic, sees many other nuances."

"Exactly, and this, Humeirah, means that the deeper the artist is, the more isolated he will be because it takes another madman to discern the additional nuances."

"Maybe it accounts for the irremovable stain of melancholia ingrained in the soul of an artist because her entire life goes in trying to communicate these feelings to other people. Most of the time she fails miserably."

"Does she?"

"Saabir, how are you?" said a voice.

Saabir stood up to greet Haider and took his hand in his.

"My sincere condolences, Haider." Haider looked at him, blinked in an affected manner, and looked away.

"I lost my daughter, Saabir. Maybe I am paying for something I did."

Humeirah looked at her husband. He glanced at her but only out of the corner of his eye. She smiled sadly to herself, remembering a conversation she had had with Vijay.

Haider continued: "Saabir, I was just about to leave. I'm sorry to be so impolite. I have a board meeting to attend in La Pirogue and I'm running late. We must meet soon."

"Go ahead, I was about to leave."

"By the way, my parents will be having a get-together to do some dua for Warissah. It will be forty days soon. That's when the soul departs. I know you don't really believe—"

"I'll be there, Haider. Count on me."

After Haider had stepped outside, Humeirah and Saabir turned to face each other. He noticed a glow on her face and attributed it to the freshness of ambition.

"I've made up my mind, Saabir, I'm not turning back. I'm leaving. I'm leaving because I have a story to tell the world."

"Are you sure? Don't you think it will be different now? Maybe the people around you will change after this event and your life will be more comfortable."

"No, Saabir. I have long believed in the ability of people to change. It doesn't work that way. I know now. I need to find out what's beyond what I have known and been confined by. I need to know so as to strengthen my opinions about the world as well as myself, and find the language to articulate and express it. Maybe someday, if or when I am ready, I will come back."

"I understand, Humeirah. I also fear that your mind and will should be dulled by the intellectual, and by that token, emotional bankruptcy of your surroundings. I wish you all the best."

Saabir stood up and moved towards the door, and as he was about to step out, he turned around. "Humeirah, take care of your eyes…"

"What do you mean?"

"Take care of your eyes, Humeirah, and return the gaze of the world that was on you with what you see and with your words…"

That afternoon, Humeirah felt something had permanently altered her perception of the world and of herself.

She imagined finding the words to express herself, so that among her readers would be those who would relate to her and understand her, and the same intimacy that bound Saabir to her heart would be established, wrapping her—and them—with the warmth of reassurance; the same that one human being longed for from another. Because she had realised that day that everyone sought just that: a connection.

# VIII

## -My Nirvana-

"We ought not be called human beings but human beasts." Humeirah

The loud voice in Humeirah's head: "Humeirah, you once ached for a direction. What have you learned?"

Humeirah: "That nobody can teach it to me. There is no single *right way*. There are only people who claim to know of it and go on to dictate it to others—to those who seek.

Yes, there is no such thing. There are only realisations which cannot be taught by others—realisations that provide a new perspective of life. The Search remains never ending, and that is the curse (or blessing?) of existence—calmness only sweeps over the seeker's soul when she learns to embrace this state of uncertainty, instability and even confusion."

The loud voice: "So what happens now?"

Humeirah: "Life goes on. The point lies in scrambling for those material and non-material things that everyone else scrambles for—because that is all we have."

The loud voice: "Hasn't your search been circular? You embarked on a search for The Truth because you were sceptical of The Scramble, and it only led you to realise that there was no constancy, stability or permanency—and no point in seeking it. Then, you understood that if there was no scramble, there was nothing else in life so that you had to reconcile yourself to it."

Humeirah: "Yes, it comes down to that. But there is a difference. My search has taught me that when I'm caught up with The Scramble, it is inevitable that I should grow weary of it time and again—that's when I've learned to stop and take a break. In the past, it was at this time that I allowed the monotony of The Scramble to torture me.

But because of the realisations I've now gained through The Search, whenever I take a break, I am not tortured, because I know that The Scramble is not everything—only an attempt to fit in and keep busy since I am here and happen to exist.

In the end I must accept myself as a mere mortal; and as needy, wanting, and insecure as every other being. And yet, strength lies in acknowledging that I must bear this burden with dignity and self-respect."

The loud voice: "So are you saying that this is *the* right way and everyone else should follow it?"

Humeirah: "No. This is only *my* way. This is the path I have chosen to reach my nirvana, and as much as I may employ words to make my thoughts known, I will never be able to guide others to where I have reached. It's been a slow and complex process—conscious and subconscious, voluntary and involuntary—of merging experience with reflection, including everything I've read, interpreted and misinterpreted. The noise as well as the silence have been as important. In other words, it's been *my* journey—no one else's. That's why I could never condemn people for their thoughts, beliefs, and, inevitably, conclusions."